Contents

Acknowledgements

Thank you first and foremost to the people who shared their time and stories with me. This book would not have been possible without you. I'm also grateful to the workers and organisations that generously and enthusiastically supported and contributed to the research.

I am grateful to Mark Peel for guiding me to transform the manuscript from a thesis to a book. Your encouragement spurred me to keep going in moments of lost confidence. Special thanks also to Eve Vincent for the stimulating discussions and feedback on drafts. There were so many times you articulated the worth of the book when I felt unable to.

I am grateful to my supervisors Amanda Wise and Raj Velayutham for the intelligent and attentive guidance throughout my PhD candidature as I conducted the research. And thank you to the other staff in the Department of Sociology at Macquarie University for always being approachable and collegial. Shaun Wilson, thanks for being my advocate and confidant.

Thank you Emma Power, Kathy Mee and Ilan Wiesel, for giving me the opportunity to put all I've learned researching and writing this book into practice again, and for creating academic care infrastructures.

Thank you to my friends who endured and supported me through the PhD and then again through drafting a book amid a pandemic and crisis in the higher education sector. Thanks to my family for never doubting me, and especially mum for your emotional investment. Zara and Antu, thank you for reminding me what's important. Adam, thank you for all the hidden intellectual, emotional and domestic support that made this book possible. Parts of the book were first published in:

Mitchell, E. (2020) 'Negotiating vulnerability: the experience of long-term social security recipients', *The Sociological Review*, 68(1): 225–241.

Mitchell, E. (2022) 'More than making do: toward a generative account of getting by on welfare benefits', *Sociology*, 56(3): 487–503.

Mitchell, E. and Vincent, E. (2021) 'The shame of welfare? Lived experiences of welfare and culturally inflected experiences of shame', *Emotion, Space and Society*, 41: 1–8.

1

Introduction: Culture matters

Hasan, a Pakistani father and husband and self-described family man, steadfastly refused to reach out for assistance with day-to-day living despite the pressure his family was under while awaiting the verdict of their asylum application. He expressed his unwillingness to claim support as a refusal despite his lack of entitlement to social security, which he dismissively lumped together with charity: 'I would rather die than I will go to a charity thing or help or grant or anything', Hasan told me.

Kat, an Aboriginal[1] woman on the Disability Support Pension (DSP), described her growing confidence dealing with welfare agencies as a strength, because 'Aboriginal people can feel more intimidated' in those situations. She was determined to impart to her teenage children a willingness to ask for help and not suffer alone: 'I think it's okay to ask for help and then that's how you learn to help yourself. I've always told the boys, "Don't ever be afraid to ask for anything".'

Jasmin, a single parent who was raised in Hong Kong, avoided telling people she received the Parenting Payment (PP), but accepted it with a stoical complacency – she'd take it if it were available, but if not, bad luck: 'If they gave me [welfare] it's a bonus, if they don't give me, that's life. That's what support should be like.'

Hasan, Kat and Jasmin (whose names have been fictionalised to protect their anonymity) were all conscious of stereotypes about asylum-seekers, Aboriginal people and single mothers as opportunistic parasites on the welfare system. And they were all struggling, albeit to different degrees, to make ends meet. Navigating the welfare system involved walking a tightrope between principles and pragmatics.

This book is about how people living at the sharp end of Australia's welfare system, like Hasan, Kat and Jasmin, negotiate the cultural assumptions and practical hurdles of contemporary social support. This is a context in which social security payments are deliberately meagre and come with strings attached and hoops to jump through; where the reigning cultural tropes of 'vulnerability' and 'personal responsibility' compel those in need to perform a balance of deference and dependence, resilience and resolve. The book problematises how welfare policy moralises the actions, life chances and choices of people receiving government income support, popularly called 'welfare' or 'the dole' in Australia. At the same time, it shows the multiple cultural resources welfare users draw on to position themselves as moral subjects in strained circumstances.

Research documenting lived experiences of welfare rarely pays sustained attention to the multicultural realities that welfare users occupy. When cultural diversity is acknowledged, understandings of culture tend to be thin, or its significance remains peripheral (Dwyer, 2000: 117; Murphy et al, 2011; Saunders, 2011). The limited attention to cultural diversity in studies of life on welfare is in part due to the warranted emphasis on shared experiences of poverty. This sentiment was expressed by one young Aboriginal man I interviewed when I explained that the aim of my research was 'to see how people from different backgrounds experience life on welfare'. He responded, dryly, 'pretty much the same I would think'. Of course, he was right. This book shows the practical and personal trials and tricks that people at the sharp end of the welfare system had in common.

However, I also show how cultural differences inflected even common experiences, illuminating the significance of particular biographies, histories and relationships to citizenship. To understand the impacts of welfare regimes on the people that use them, we need to listen to diverse voices in a way that neither smooths over nor reifies differences. For one thing, given the cultural complexity that characterises social life in an age of globalisation, exploring how social rights are read and experienced through cultural frames will help us better understand what public assistance and social citizenship mean to people in their everyday lives (Shaver, 2007). A sustained and nuanced examination of cultural diversity is also necessary if we are to explain how culture matters, and is made to matter, in contemporary social policy. Only then can we challenge the cultural stereotypes that frame welfare policy and politics (Lamont and Small, 2008).

Australia provides a unique vantage point to explore these issues. It is a settler-colonial nation federated on the principles of white supremacy and protectionism (Atkinson, 2017) that has branded itself as 'the most successful multicultural country in the world' (Australian Government, 2018: 3). The questions of belonging and entitlement that underpin social citizenship are haunted by Indigenous dispossession and sovereignty (Moreton-Robinson, 2003) and the persistent socio-economic marginalisation of Indigenous peoples and minority ethnic groups. The Australian context brings into sharp relief the legacy and continuity of racial and socio-economic inequalities that underlie the tension between principles of protection and empowerment, difference and equality. This tension also plays out across other predominantly English-speaking democracies with relatively low spending and targeted welfare systems that are grappling with waning faith in traditional welfare models amid economic uncertainty and increasing cultural diversity.

Living social policy

While conducting this research, I would routinely travel the 30 minutes or so from my home in the gentrified, mainly English-speaking, inner western suburbs of Sydney to the super-diverse southwest, where my research was based. On one of my journeys west, I overheard a Sydney-sider boast that we were entering 'Sydney's underbelly'. The growth of Lebanese and Vietnamese settlements and the decline of manufacturing in Sydney's southwest since the 1980s has been used as media fodder for sensationalist stories of crime, unemployment and religious extremism. I had grown up further west in a regional town also hollowed out by the decline of manufacturing and heavy industry, but without the immigrant profile or racialised reputation of my research site.

On one occasion, a train carried me home after I had spent the morning volunteering at a family support programme and an afternoon interviewing Monica, an Anglo single parent who had been on welfare for most of her adult life. 'What gives us the right?' Monica had asked rhetorically about living on public assistance paid for by working taxpayers. I recorded my conflicted feelings on my phone as I travelled home after talking to her at length:

FIELD NOTES
12 March 2015

I really do feel she judges herself and others too harshly. But I'm also uncomfortable, despite my reflexes, with reducing her world view to internalised myths about lazy people who just don't want to work. I, like her, have repeatedly experienced and witnessed people making choices that worsen their situations. But I'm still convinced (or perhaps I'm trying to convince myself and it is my doubt that is unsettling) that those poor decisions derive from a sense of limited options (horizons) and limited capacity fostered through circumstance.

I could see myself in her fierce commitment to family and pained desire to make their lives better despite their circumstances and, sometimes, themselves. As if to underline the point, my attempt to jot down field notes on my phone was repeatedly interrupted by the alert of incoming calls. I ignored the first six, knowing it was my brother pestering me for money after spending the last of his welfare payment. At last I answered, deciding I could spare the money regardless of what he would spend it on. More importantly, it was worth giving my parents some reprieve from the same barrage of calls without the income to match.

In this book I try to preserve the complexity and vivacity of lived lives in my retelling of them. I offer an ethnographic account of life at the sharp end of

Australia's welfare system in a region of Sydney known for its concentration of socio-economic disadvantage and ethnic diversity. Ethnographic research tries to get close to everyday life as it unfolds and as it is understood by the people living it. It revels in the human side of research and does not shy away from contradiction. I spent 18 months between January 2014 and June 2015 volunteering in a local community welfare organisation, observing support programmes, and interviewing 11 community welfare workers and a mix of 25 residents receiving some form of income support. This included people who relied on welfare payments to stay afloat, people who pieced together a living from a combination of income support and paid work, as well as people struggling to get by who refused or were ineligible for assistance. Throughout the book I use the term 'welfare users' rather than the more common 'welfare recipients' to position people who access welfare as actively participating in survival and care by claiming assistance (Dwyer, 2000).

This book also works against either 'welfare user' or 'welfare recipient' as the defining category of people's lives. People are not one-dimensional, and nor should stories of their life be. I am inspired by the writing of Melissa Lucashenko (2013), Lisa McKenzie (2015), Eve Vincent (2023) and Mark Peel (2003). The approach of the book reflects my academic training as a sociologist of everyday life and my personal experience of growing up in a poor, white family reliant on welfare. Many of my immediate and extended family members still rely on welfare and, while the upward mobility afforded by working in academia means I am more comfortable and secure than I have ever been, I am still embroiled in the mundane drama of their poverty. I feel keenly the responsibility to neither turn away from the damage expressed in people's stories nor reduce their stories to damage (Tuck, 2009). My personal experiences and scholarly influences make me sensitive to the messiness and ambiguity that are often missing from sympathetic and cynical accounts of life on welfare.

The book also works against the presumption that 'culture' is the terrain of minority 'others' and 'diversity' is code for 'different from the dominant norm'. I ask, how do different ways of doing obligation in a multicultural, settler-colony like Australia rub up against the cultural assumptions embedded in welfare arrangements? I explore the cultural resources minority ethnic, Indigenous *and* Anglo welfare users draw on to make sense of, and make their way through, the Australian welfare system. Foregrounding diverse stories told from different social locations thwarts any simplistic identification I might have with the people involved in the research despite my own personal experience. I share the stories peopled shared with me as an outsider to the area and from my vantage point as a researcher.

I refer to Australia's welfare system often as shorthand for the aggregate of public agencies, non-profit and private organisations responsible for delivering social services while governments set standards and control the purse strings. This reflects the lay language of the conversations I had, as well as allowing me to trace broad trends in policy approaches. I am aware, however, that talking about 'the welfare system' or 'welfare state' collapses a complex mix of purposes, arrangements and players into an apparently single and coherent entity (Clarke, 2004). In a fragmented welfare landscape, the places and provisions that make social citizenship an everyday reality for people on the ground are various and uneven.

Moving social policy

Contemporary welfare politics trades in morally potent and contested ideas about vulnerability and responsibility (Brown et al, 2017). The malleability of these concepts means they can stand for divergent visions of the welfare system (Brown, 2011), whether that be an emphasis on personal responsibility and limiting the role of government, the principle of social justice secured by the state, or placing responsibility for prevention and intervention in the community and generalist services such as schools. Labels of vulnerability are associated with the identification of groups deemed to have complex needs that require pre-emptive intervention, including Indigenous peoples and minority ethnic populations (Best, 2013; Stinson, 2019; Stanley and De Froideville, 2020). As anthropologist Catherine Kingfisher (2013: 6, 14) theorises, policy ideas travel 'across geographic and cultural space', combining and recombining with what is known and practised locally to form culturally and historically rooted iterations. Tracing the international dominance of ideas of vulnerability and personal responsibility in social policy, then, involves attending to how the meaning of these terms 'shifts across time and space' (Kingfisher, 2013: 13).

When I began my PhD in late 2012, compulsory income management had recently been introduced to Bankstown in southwest Sydney. The welfare quarantining measure seizes a percentage of a recipient's welfare payments onto an electronic card to ensure it is spent on essential items. The policy experiment originally affected remote-living Aboriginal people exclusively, and required the suspension of the 1975 Racial Discrimination Act (RDA). The measure was a cornerstone of the Northern Territory National Emergency Response (NTER) announced by the federal coalition government in 2007. The Intervention, as it was popularly known, revived public and academic debate about whether poor health and poverty among Aboriginal people had cultural or colonialist roots (Walter, 2009).

The movement of income management from remote Aboriginal Australia to multicultural metropolitan Sydney brought into relief how the cultural politics of welfare interact with lived diversity. Bankstown was one of five locations across urban and regional Australia designated a 'disadvantaged area' under the new policy of 'place-based income management'. By this time, compulsory income management had been reframed as a welfare rather than Indigenous policy issue. 'Vulnerable welfare payment recipients' were defined in legislation as triggering compulsory income management in designated locations (Bielefeld, 2018). In the early days of the place-based trial, local opponents argued that Bankstown was being targeted because of its reputation as an enclave of ethnic conflict, and that it would restrict migrant communities' access to traditional foods and the ability to send remittances to support family overseas (Marks, 2012).

By 2014, when I began my fieldwork, compulsory income management had not taken off in Bankstown to the extent policymakers expected or opponents worried it would. But the corrupting influence of welfare payments was still in the spotlight. My first interview coincidently took place a matter of days after the controversial and unpopular 2014 Federal Budget was announced. Treasurer Joe Hockey declared the federal government's intention to make major changes to the welfare system, including time-limited benefits for the unemployed, added work-related conditions for young people receiving unemployment payments and disability pensions, tightened eligibility for pensions and family payments, and a co-payment for Medicare (Australia's universal health insurance system). The epochal tone heralded a new era of personal responsibility, sacrifice and contribution that would sustain a welfare system reserved for 'those in genuine need', 'the most disadvantaged' and 'the most vulnerable' (Hockey, 2014). It was a matter not just of financial prudence, but moral obligation. Critics responded with accusations that the government was 'attacking the most vulnerable' through harsh welfare reforms, and failing in its responsibility to protect those in need.

It was against the backdrop of this announcement that I asked people living in or on the edges of hardship to reflect on their experiences and expectations of informal and formal social support. Public debates about what we want our welfare system to look like, what is fair and who should benefit from welfare loomed large in the interviews. While many of the proposed changes were defeated in Parliament, since then the screws have continued to tighten on conditions and sanctions for single parents and people with disabilities, while access to welfare has further narrowed for migrants. Meanwhile, trials of the most restrictive and punitive programmes have continued to disproportionately effect Indigenous welfare users (Klein, 2021: 44). I document these changes, placing them in global context, in Chapter 2.

Almost a decade after beginning my PhD, I wrote this Introduction as Sydney emerged from an outbreak of the Delta variant of COVID-19 and a three-month lockdown that hit residents of southwest and western Sydney the hardest. The residents of these areas were portrayed in the media and political commentary as disproportionately vulnerable to COVID-19 *and* as a risk to the wider collective. These are areas where bigger families tend to live in smaller homes, where extended family stretches across households, where more people work in insecure and lower paid jobs, and where essential workers who cannot work from home are concentrated. In public commentary about the outbreak, attributing transmissions to larger households and insecure work became code for blaming different cultural groups for the failure to contain the outbreak (Carrigan, 2021). Whether ways of getting through the lockdown were the product of cultural differences or socio-economic inequalities again became a point of debate.

As in other countries around the world, the pandemic laid bare existing inequalities; disadvantaged areas endured many more COVID-19 cases, extra lockdown restrictions and heavy-handed police and military enforcement of stay-at-home orders. Socially and economically disadvantaged areas, including southwest Sydney, where the research for this book was based, saw the largest and most lingering increase of people relying on welfare (Davidson et al, 2021). The first wave of the pandemic in Australia saw the number of people on the lowest welfare payments increase by 70 per cent to 2,221,000 (Davidson et al, 2021). Many Australians who had never had to deal with the lumbering bureaucracy of Centrelink (the government agency that oversees the distribution of statutory income support programmes) suddenly relied on it to keep them afloat.

The federal government's response to the first lockdown in March 2020 effectively doubled the most meagre welfare payments as the welfare rolls swelled. In contrast, eligibility for the place-based COVID-19 Disaster Payment was decidedly narrower than when the pandemic first ground public life to a halt. The federal government introduced the payment during the Delta outbreak to compensate for loss of income resulting from lockdowns. Welfare recipients were initially ineligible for the COVID-19 Disaster Payment and later could only access the $200-per-week if they could show they had lost at least 8 hours of work. After providing a glimpse of a genuinely supportive social security system, the federal government had reverted to its begrudging approach. I return to this point in Chapter 8.

Roadmap to the book

Readers interested in the more conceptual and technical aspects of the research design will find more details in Appendix A. Appendix B provides a table of Australian income support payments when I undertook the fieldwork, and in 2022 at the time of writing.

Chapter 2 provides the big picture backdrop for the rest of the book by placing Australia's welfare system in historical and international context.

Chapter 3 looks at the different versions of reciprocity that the welfare users I interviewed drew on to frame and justify their expectations of social support. Familiar scripts are loaded with the details of personal biography and social circumstance.

Chapter 4 focuses on interviews with frontline workers in the community welfare sector. It shows how ideas about positive and negative access inform judgements about the 'deserving vulnerability' and 'empowered responsibility' of welfare users.

Chapter 5 foregrounds the experiences of the most marginal welfare claimants in my study. It shows they are often required to reperform vulnerability for the welfare system, some choosing to remove themselves from the welfare rolls rather than make themselves vulnerable again to the audience of experts.

Chapter 6 looks closely at the stories of two individuals in very different circumstances, but both afflicted with a deep sense of shame about relying on the Australian government for help. Asserting the power of personal choice as a vehicle for change and the sacrifice of personal dignity for the survival of the family is an anguished strategy of self-preservation when the prospects of one's family look bleak and uncertain.

Chapter 7 draws attention to the modest pursuits and pleasures that sustain a liveable life in hardship but don't necessarily conform to popular ideas of 'good resilience'.

Chapter 8 concludes by reflecting on the potential for a welfare system that creates possibilities rather than problems for those who rely on it.

2

A hand up, not a handout

The phrase 'a hand up, not a handout' has long been used to sum up a model of welfare that aims to curb social spending and cultivate hard-working citizens who can take care of themselves. In 2019, former Australian coalition prime minister, Scott Morrison, wheeled out the phrase to celebrate the success of more than two decades of welfare-to-work policy in Australia (Curtis, 2019). He pointed to evidence not of poor Australians living better lives, but of the number of people who had dropped off the welfare rolls and the number of penalties that had been issued by welfare agencies. The country's lowest payments, Newstart Allowance (NSA) and Youth Allowance (YA), had not increased in real terms in over 20 years. But the requirements and sanctions attached to payments had become more far-reaching and stringent over this time. The Morrison government seemed more committed to doling out moral and monetary punishment than lifting people out of poverty.

Two decades earlier, British prime minister at the time, Tony Blair, used the phrase to sum up a different way of doing welfare that promoted individual responsibility and opportunity above rights and protection (White, 1999). This was sold as a 'third way' between the post-war protective welfare state and a hands-off neoliberal approach (Giddens, 1998). The aim of social welfare thus shifts from expensive redistribution to productive investment in the capacities of citizens, transforming welfare states from 'safety nets into springboards' (Best, 2013: 110). Poverty is reimagined as vulnerability and multifaceted exclusion from the mainstream; complex problems are said to require dynamic and pro-active interventions that provide short-term relief and change individual behaviour to make citizens more resilient in the long term. In this context, community is positioned as better suited to respond to the diverse needs and preferences of individuals without the State stifling their independence.

The idea that public benefits and services should come with strings attached to mould the behaviour of recipients has taken hold across the global North and South, although the tone and shape of policies varies across time and place (Dwyer, 2019). In high-income, predominantly English-speaking countries with advanced welfare states, these ideas are tied to the argument that 'passive' welfare breeds inactivity and irresponsibility and entrenches welfare dependency. Welfare dependency rhetoric discredits the post-Second World War emphasis on welfare rights as financially unsustainable and morally hazardous.

While concern about the morally corrupting effects of welfare provision reach further back, it was revived in the late 1980s and spread in the 1990s when North American scholars and politicians blamed welfare benefits for creating a 'culture of dependency' that perpetuates poverty (Mead, 1986; Murray, 1990). They argued that poor people live according to a distinct subculture of dysfunctional values and behaviours that is passed down through welfare-dependent families. These arguments relied on and rejuvenated racial stereotypes about the family practices and work proclivities of African Americans (Fraser and Gordon, 1994). Rather than withdrawing public support altogether, influential reformer Lawrence Mead (1997) argued that welfare could be reshaped as a corrective tool to bring the values and behaviour of the poor in line with the mainstream. This required supervising the lives of the poor more closely and dictating how they behave as a condition of receiving public support. This model of welfare is paternalist because it assumes government knows best how welfare recipients should behave. It is different from older forms of paternalism because it aims to shape the behaviour of individuals as they go about their life rather than in the confinement of institutions.

Welfare dependency rhetoric builds on a long tradition of branding recipients of poor relief as lazy and deficient, rooted in the legacy of the British Poor Laws. In the settler-colonies of Australia, Aotearoa/New Zealand and Canada, it is also shaped by racial politics of white nation-building in relationship to immigration and Indigenous sovereignty. The association between Indigenous peoples and welfare dependency is embedded in a history of using welfare measures to make Indigenous populations more like the colonising culture (Humpage, 2010; Papillon, 2015). As the speed and scale of international migration grows, the singling out of migrant and refugee welfare dependency is tied to public rhetoric about opportunistic asylum-seekers and undeserving migrants. Possessive anxieties about bloated welfare rolls and porous borders are, of course, not unique to the settler-colonies. In the UK, for example, they come together in racist depictions of Roma as 'benefit tourists' (Dinu and Scullion, 2019: 124).

A model of citizenship and welfare that prioritises behavioural obligations focuses attention on 'the cultural dimension of conduct and belonging' and positions cultural difference as a potential subversion that needs to be brought in line (Flint, 2009: 92). The next section outlines how these ideas have helped reshape the Australian welfare system over the last three decades prior to the defeat of Scott Morrison in the May 2022 federal election, which ended nine years of coalition government. But welfare states have always been shaped by cultural assumptions about gender and race that bolster some forms of work and family life as the norm. Tracing the longer history of how the Australian welfare system has dealt with Indigenous and minority ethnic others allows us to appraise the shortfalls of contemporary policy without romanticising the protective post-war welfare state or its modest provisions and exclusions. The chapter concludes by situating major changes in Australia in relation to key developments in Aotearoa/New Zealand, Canada and the UK.

Lean and mean welfare in 21st-century Australia

Neoliberal reforms have reshaped rather than replaced Australia's social security system (Spies-Butcher, 2014). Neoliberalism generally refers to a set of ideals and practices favouring market competition over state intervention, emphasising individual choice and freedom. It is more akin to a 'toolbox' of strategies associated with these ideals than a single or deliberate policy agenda (Strakosch, 2015: 79). Australia began neoliberal reforms to its social security system comparatively early (Considine, 2001). For-profit and non-profit organisations already had an established role in social welfare, but since the 1980s Australia has led experiments in more radical models of privatised service delivery (Wright et al, 2011: 301). A large range of publicly funded profit and non-profit providers administers the supports and sanctions of an increasingly conditional social security system. Despite the rhetoric of reigning in welfare budgets, government spending on health and family payments has grown, and continues to maintain the real income of many poor Australians (Mendes, 2009: 109). But new spending has been directly linked to reforms that have reduced wages and made employment more insecure (Spies-Butcher, 2014).

'Income support payments' have always been strictly means- and asset-tested in Australia to keep welfare spending low and targeted (Wilson et al, 2013). Australian citizens and permanent residents who meet certain criteria may qualify for a range of payments, including those reserved for low-income parents, the unemployed, people with disabilities, young people and the aged. But repeated reforms have tightened eligibility and ramped up the conditions attached to payments. 'Work first' policies have been widened to include all working-age benefit claimants. Conditions initially associated with finding work have spread into the sphere of parenting (Taylor et al, 2016).

In Australia, both sides of government have borrowed from the toolbox of neoliberalism. The Hawke/Keating Labor governments began in the late 1980s by introducing compulsory 'activity tests' for the unemployed and promoting 'reciprocal obligation' in the *Working Nation* package. From 1996 the Liberal–National coalition government, led by John Howard, embraced and extended 'mutual obligation' policies at the same time as outsourcing employment services and increasing the role of charities in welfare delivery. The Howard government argued that the long-term unemployed owed a debt to society, which could be repaid by attending 'work for the dole', work-ready training or voluntary community service.

Migrant access to social security has also become increasingly restricted and differentiated by payment type and visa status (Boucher, 2014). A 'user pays' approach to immigration began in the late 1980s, with the introduction in the early 1990s of mandatory sponsorship bonds to bring parents to Australia and a six-month waiting period before newly arrived migrants, except for humanitarian visa holders, could access unemployment payments (Boucher, 2014: 372). Since 1996, waiting periods have been extended to more payment types and have become increasingly drawn out, while the cost of sponsorship bonds and visas has soared. Meanwhile, people seeking asylum in Australia can only apply for discretionary financial assistance typically set at 89% of the lowest welfare payments. Eligibility is determined by the Department of Home Affairs and has tightened considerably in recent years (van Kooy and Ward, 2019).

While 'conditional citizenship' takes back pre-existing entitlements for failing to meet obligations, making migrants prove self-reliance for a period before they can claim social support suggests that citizenship must be 'earned' in advance (Flint, 2009: 89). These shifts also draw family obligations into the regulation of immigrant welfare by insisting on familial responsibility for care (Boucher, 2014: 369). This relates to a wider problem of assuming that minority ethnic families have extended family and community networks that fill the gap of formal support, which is contradicted by research (see, for example, Cardona et al, 2006; Atkin and Chattoo, 2007).

Successive governments have followed down this path of tightening eligibility and increasing conditionality. Labor governments have been more inclined to endorse conditional welfare in the name of egalitarian goals, while Liberal–National governments have been more stridently punitive in approach. But both major political parties have entrenched policies that scrutinise and target individual behaviour on the grounds that welfare dependency is the problem and paid work is the solution.

Since I conducted my fieldwork in 2014–15, Australia's social security system has only become harsher. From March 2020, several allowances, including unemployment benefit and non-work benefits, have been collapsed into a single JobSeeker Payment (JSP). Measuring the JSP rate as a proportion of the country's average wage, Australia had until very recently the lowest payment in the Organisation for Ecomonic Co-operation and Development, even after Rent Assistance was added. After increasing the payment by $50 per fortnight, it is now the second lowest (Whiteford and Bradbury, 2021). The justification is that keeping payments painfully low creates a disincentive to stay on welfare and an incentive to look for and take work. The reality is that making life hard on welfare makes it harder to find work (Morris et al, 2015). While making welfare recipients jump through more hoops for lower payments may divert people from the welfare rolls, this does not mean they have been able to find or keep work (Watts and Fitzpatrick, 2018: 8).

And yet, welfare policy remains fixated on 'work first' and uninterested in the inhospitable job market or competing responsibilities that get in the way of work. During the period of my fieldwork, eligibility for the Disability Support Pension (DSP) was tightened further and the assessment process became even more demanding (Soldadic et al, 2021). Applicants deemed capable of working 15–29 hours per week are no longer eligible for DSP and have been pushed onto much lower payments with 'mutual obligations' attached (Soldadic et al, 2021: 13). Parenting Payment (PP) recipients (mainly single parents) have also been moved onto the lower unemployment benefit (formerly Newstart, now JSP), and made to look for work when their youngest child reaches school age.

Indigenous communities have borne the brunt of social experiments targeting conditional welfare policies at 'vulnerable groups'. Culture of poverty arguments fuse with the denigration of Aboriginal cultural practices as deficient and in need of remedial intervention (Walter, 2009). Aboriginal welfare recipients in remote communities have been subject to more demanding work-for-the-dole requirements and more frequent penalties (Fowkes, 2019). Policies controlling how income support payments are spent were first applied exclusively to remote Aboriginal communities in the Northern Territory, requiring the suspension of the 1975 Racial Discrimination Act (RDA). In Australia, these major changes to the welfare system were explicitly framed 'within a wider "race" debate about Indigenous dysfunction' that paved the way for their incremental spread to other welfare recipients and new locales (Humpage, 2010: 525–6).

Since 2016, after my fieldwork, the scrutiny and selection of groups at risk of welfare dependency has become more technical with the rise of big data (Staines et al, 2021). Following in the footsteps of Aotearoa/New Zealand, the Morrison coalition government revived a version of social investment geared towards future payoffs in reduced welfare spending. Unlike earlier Labor-led approaches to social investment in both countries, the latest version is devoid of any acknowledgement of structural disadvantage (Humpage et al, 2020: 10). In Australia, key target groups have included 'young carers, young parents, students, older unemployed people, working-age refugees and migrants, working-age carers and "at risk young people"' (Staines et al, 2021: 164). The McClure Review of Australia's welfare and employment services system – set up by the coalition government elected in 2013 – justifies the need for 'individualised and intensive investment' in terms of doing more to enable vulnerable groups to 'achieve self-reliance and live a life they value' (McClure Review, 2015: 127). But a life of value is still reduced to the benefits of paid work, and policy remains focused on changing 'problem' behaviours.

White man's welfare in the 20th century

Moral distinctions between the 'deserving' and 'undeserving' poor may have returned to prominence over the last three decades, but they are deeply rooted in the foundations of the Australian welfare state. The two largest colonies in Australia, New South Wales and Victoria, set up Old Age Pensions in 1900, paving the way for the Invalid and Old-age Pensions Act in 1908. The pension was framed as a right for those who had given a lifetime of 'service' through work, but it could still be denied to individuals if they were deemed immoral. The legislation included a 'good character' requirement, and it explicitly excluded most non-white residents (Smyth, 2011: 181).

Australia, like its neighbour Aotearoa/New Zealand, focused on 'making work pay' (Smyth, 2011: 180) to improve living standards, reserving public assistance for those outside of the job market. This antipodean model is referred to as a 'wage earners' welfare state' (Castles, 1996). The centrepiece of this approach in Australia was the Harvester Judgement, which bound employers to pay a male worker enough to support himself and his dependent family to live in 'frugal comfort' (Murphy, 2011: 87). The 'average' family envisioned by Judge Higgins was made up of a male breadwinner, a woman responsible for maintaining the home, and two or three children. Aboriginal people were explicitly excluded from the first industrial awards (Altman and Sanders, 1991: 2). Meanwhile, the White Australia policy restricted immigration and protected white workers from low wages and unemployment by keeping non-white workers out.

A separate system nominally concerned with the 'welfare' of Aboriginal people controlled all aspects of their daily life (Vincent, 2021: 4). Protectionism was the official policy for managing Aboriginal people in the latter decades of the 19th century and early decades of the 20th century. All Australian states passed legislation, known as the Protection Acts, that gave a Protection Board and Chief Protectors extensive powers to control the movement and property of Aboriginal people, including in some states and the Northern Territory the legal guardianship of all Aboriginal children. In reality the everyday management and supervision of Aboriginal people fell on missionaries and employers of poorly paid or unpaid Aboriginal workers (Altman and Sanders, 1991).

The language of 'welfare' was increasingly used from the 1930s when the goal of policy shifted to 'assimilation'. Assimilation was a deliberate strategy of absorbing mixed-descent Aboriginal people into the white population by targeting children to 'breed out the colour' and 'teach away the culture' (Altman and Sanders, 1991). The forcible removal of Aboriginal children from their families later came to be known as the 'Stolen Generations'. Proponents of assimilation framed it as 'advancement' and preparation for future citizenship. These ideas also influenced Aboriginal activists and their supporters in their growing call for equal rights (Atwood and Markus, 1999). Demands for equality, particularly from the 1930s, developed the conditions for the constitutional referendum in 1967 that brought Aboriginal affairs under the remit of the Commonwealth and counted Aboriginal people as citizens.

Australia's safety net widens (for some)

Social assistance expanded in the 1940s but it was far from universal. Wartime (1939–45) allowed the Labor government to take control of income taxation powers necessary to fund social security payments from general revenue (Thornton et al, 2020). By the end of the war, the Child Endowment (1941), Widow's Pension (1943) and Unemployment and Sickness Benefit (1944) were in place and included character tests. Unemployment benefits were framed as a reward for hard work rather than a handout (Thornton et al, 2020: 5). Unlike the UK, which was busy building a comprehensive welfare state, the emphasis in Australia was still on the relatively generous work arrangements and commitment to creating full employment. But the UK model would come to influence the post-war development of social policy in the settler colonies of Australia, Aotearoa/New Zealand and Canada (Smyth, 2011).

The ideal of the white nuclear family prevailed in this period. Married women were not eligible for the unemployment benefit unless they could show that their husbands could not 'maintain' them (Harris, 2001: 13). Recognising the need for more workers and consumers to fuel post-war reconstruction, the Labor government relaxed immigration restrictions to allow Europeans in (Jakubowicz, 1989: 2). But the preference was still to attract people from the British Isles, and social security provisions were initially limited to British Commonwealth immigrants. White women were encouraged to return to their primary role as wives and mothers after the war, replaced by migrant men in construction and heavy metal industries and migrant women in the factories (Jakubowicz, 1989: 3–4).

Social security was one of the first areas where 'conditional inclusion' in the emerging welfare state was extended to Aboriginal people (Murphy, 2013). Individuals could access benefits if they were exempted from the State and Territory legal definitions of Aboriginality, or if their 'character, standard of intelligence, and social development' made granting eligibility 'reasonable' (Altman and Sanders, 1991: 3). Social security legislation also allowed Aboriginal welfare authorities to receive benefits instead of paying them directly to individuals (Altman and Sanders, 1991: 3). For a large part of the 20th century support was provided to Aboriginal people in the form of rations administered not only by officials, but also missionaries, miners and pastoralists (Rowse, 1998: 4). Rations were used as a tool of assimilation to reform Indigenous behaviours and families in preparation for the transition to citizenship and the cash economy (Rowse, 1998: 3).

The idea of universal welfare rights guaranteed by the state did not take off in Australia until the 1960s. During this period recruitment of immigrant workers for manufacturing extended to Malta, Germany, Italy, Greece, Yugoslavia, Turkey and Lebanon (Jakubowicz, 1989: 4). Social movements for gender equity, multiculturalism and Indigenous rights pushed for a more expansive idea of social rights at the same time as challenging mono-cultural visions of equality. The short-lived Whitlam Labor government (1972–75) made dramatic changes: legislating equal access to social security and award wages, raising the unemployment benefit, extending the Age Pension to all Australians over 70 and establishing universal social services such as healthcare (Thornton et al, 2020: 15).

Economic downturn and growing unemployment, borne largely by poorly paid migrant and Indigenous workers, had chipped away at the conviction that full employment and fair wages would substitute for a welfare state. But changing economic conditions also meant that the vision of a universal and expansive Australian welfare state was mired in concern about economic sustainability from the outset. The Fraser coalition government, elected in 1975 after the dismissal of Whitlam, kept some of Whitlam's reforms but reasserted social welfare as a last resort for those most in need. Fraser watered down, and then reversed, Whitlam's universal health insurance scheme; a revised version of universal health insurance was not reinstated until 1984 as part of a trade-off for economic restructuring.

Dealing with cultural difference

The guiding principles of multiculturalism and Indigenous self-determination emerged in parallel but have tended to be kept separate in Australian intellectual and public debate. This is the legacy of a longstanding treatment of Indigenous affairs and Indigenous–State relationships as a separate sphere since the 19th century. It also reflects historical and continuing distinctions in thinking about race that assumes non-white 'others' occupy a continuum from black to white (Curthoys, 2000). Multiculturalism's association with nation-building also conflicted with emerging assertions of Aboriginal nationhood (Moran, 2017). Indigenous peoples are not one group within a diverse society, but hold special claims based on continuing sovereignty (Moreton-Robinson, 2003).

The Whitlam Labor government was strongly influenced by demands for minority rights, and introduced formal policies of Indigenous self-determination and multiculturalism. While Indigenous and multicultural issues were kept separate, Whitlam formed the Department of Aboriginal Affairs (DAA) and migrant units were set up in within the Departments of

Social Security, Health and Education to encourage inclusive State welfare policies. Whitlam insisted that government agencies and departments should be doing more for Aboriginal people and migrants from non-English-speaking backgrounds, at the same time as promoting Aboriginal-specific assistance programmes and ethnic welfare organisations (Jakubowicz, 1989: 11; Altman and Sanders, 1991: 5–7). A tension between mainstream and specialised services emerged at this time.

In the formative years of multicultural policy, both sides of government relied on an ethnic group model of welfare but from different angles. The Whitlam Labor government perceived migrants as a 'disadvantaged group' that ought to be targeted by specific social welfare programmes (Moran, 2017: 37). Fraser framed multiculturalism in terms of cultural recognition and social cohesion rather than systemic inequalities. Ethnic service delivery fitted his preference for residual welfare because it promoted volunteerism, communal responsibility and competition for resources among organisations (Walsh, 2014: 286). The 'ethnicity model' drew increasing criticism for its inferior services, for treating 'culture' as the cause of disadvantage and dysfunction, and ignoring other unequal power relations such as class and gender (Vasta, 2004: 201).

Multicultural policy turned toward mainstreaming in the 1980s under the rationale of redirecting scarce resources to core programmes (Jakubowicz, 1989: 13). The Hawke Labor government adopted the Access and Equity Strategy, which aimed to equip government services with the capacity to meet diverse needs and consult with ethnic groups about how best to meet their needs (Koleth, 2010: 11). It was originally focused on immigrants but then expanded to include 'anyone who may face barriers because of race, culture, religion, language or Indigenous background' (Moran, 2017: 95). The Hawke government also created the Aboriginal and Torres Strait Islander Commission (ATSIC) in 1989, a national body with the dual functions of administering programmes and advising government. Whether ATSIC amounted to an advancement of self-determination, as the Hawke government promoted it, was highly debated. However, its creation enabled the substantial growth and spread of the Community Development Employment Project (CDEP) scheme, which funded Indigenous community councils or incorporated organisations to pay employees a wage equivalent to income support payments to work in locally prioritised roles (Jordan and Altman, 2016).

The Howard coalition government that came to power in 1996 rejected multiculturalism and self-determination. It continued mainstreaming by reducing the budget of ethnic- and immigration-based organisations and Indigenous-specific programmes. The Howard government favoured temporary visas that denied the rights associated with permanent settlement and restricted access to social security for newly arrived migrants (Koleth,

2010: 13; Walsh, 2014: 289). Howard also dismissed any semblance of political redress as a goal of Indigenous social policy, and foregrounded material disadvantage instead (Strakosch, 2015: 77).

The paternalism that had receded with the rise of self-determination as the dominant principle guiding Indigenous affairs again took centre stage (Sanders, 2008). Alongside the thinking of Lawrence Mead, the writing of Guugu Yimithirr[1] lawyer and high-profile social commentator, Noel Pearson (2000), strongly influenced welfare reform at the turn of the century. Pearson argued that it was not absence of rights but an absence of responsibility that was causing social breakdown in remote Aboriginal communities, which worsened when equal access to social security and award wages resulted in soaring unemployment and reliance on 'passive' welfare. Pearson's critique heralded the sweeping changes introduced as part of the Northern Territory Emergency Response (NTER) launched by the Commonwealth government in 2007 in response to reports of child abuse in remote Aboriginal communities. Compulsory income management was introduced alongside alcohol bans, the compulsory acquisition of Aboriginal lands and reforms to the governance of Aboriginal organisations (Watson, 2010). Soon after, the CDEP scheme was abolished because payments could not be quarantined if they were wages. This aligned with high-profile criticism, including from Pearson, that the scheme consisted of glorified welfare payments rather than 'real work' (Jordan and Altman, 2016: 7).

The direction of welfare, immigration and Indigenous policy has not altered course in the 21st century. The Rudd and Gillard Labor governments (2007–13) changed their language but maintained many of the policies they inherited from the coalition government. After defeating the coalition in the 2007 federal election, the Rudd government rebranded the NTER measures as part of the 'Close the Gap' targets to improve Indigenous health, education and employment outcomes. Despite the language of 'partnership' across levels of government and with Indigenous stakeholders, ideas of policy failure and change still dominated, and the pursuit of socio-economic equality at the expense of valuing Indigenous diversity and difference remained (Sanders and Hunt, 2010: 225). Labor also revived a celebratory multicultural rhetoric of respect and harmony, but did not significantly reverse the regression of federal multicultural policy that took place during the Howard years (Tavan, 2012: 556–7). Coalition governments since 2013 have largely replicated the chauvinist stance of the Howard government.

The many faces of mean welfare

An overview of historical through-lines and major shifts in welfare provision can smooth over the contestation and contradiction that shapes living policy.

For one thing, welfare scholars have long highlighted the coexistence of caring and controlling imperatives in welfare provision (Piven and Cloward, 1972). This is heightened in mixed welfare economies in which governments have less direct involvement in service delivery. Inadequate payments and intensive targeting of groups deemed 'vulnerable' draws welfare users increasingly into the orbit of charities, non-profit community organisations and for-profit service providers (O'Sullivan et al, 2021; Parsell et al, 2022). Welfare policy has many faces that are not uniform across places or populations. In this final section, I trace some broad international connections and divergences across the settler-colonies of Australia, Aotearoa/New Zealand and Canada, which share 'mutually constitutive colonial histories' with the UK (Mills and Klein, 2021: 339).

The UK, Canada and Aotearoa/New Zealand have moved in a similar direction to Australia with increasingly strict requirements and severe sanctions applied to unemployment and non-work-related payments (Pierson and Humpage, 2016). Reform in Aotearoa/New Zealand has been less consistent, with the National government's decisive tightening of eligibility and ramping up of work obligations across the 1990s wound back by the Labour government that came to power in 1999 (Pierson and Humpage, 2016: 270). The difference narrowed under the conservative National-led government (2008–17), which introduced new conditions and sanctions, many of which remain in place (Gray, 2019). The rise of 'work first' policies in Canada is associated with the devolution of social services to the provinces in 1996. Centralised funding was cut back, requiring provinces to contribute more, and national standards were abandoned except for residency requirements (Kingfisher, 2013: 34). The provinces are responsible for 'setting their own benefit rates, eligibility restrictions and policies' (Hillel, 2020: 42). Ontario, British Columbia and Alberta especially have cut social programmes, contracted to private providers and introduced welfare-to-work policies. The UK has gone a step further by extending behavioural conditions and sanctions to benefit claimants working in low-paid jobs (Dwyer and Wright, 2014).

Major immigrant-receiving countries use immigration laws as well as welfare laws to limit migrant social rights (Boucher, 2014: 269). In the UK, the 1971 Immigration Act required all new migrants to support themselves as a condition of entry, including Commonwealth citizens who previously had the same rights as UK citizens (Shutes, 2016: 669). More recently, the UK has followed Australia by adopting a points-based immigration system that ranks the skill and income of migrants and limits their access to social security, while seeking to deter asylum-seekers by imposing destitution (Mills and Klein, 2021: 400, 408). A separate system of support for asylum-seekers is delivered via vouchers and a cashless payment card in the UK, and is conditional on accepting dispersed accommodation (Mills and Klein,

2021: 411). In Canada, restrictions to sponsored (family) new migrants' access to social assistance vary across provinces, but no provinces restrict access for economic migrants like Australia (Boucher, 2014: 374).

Australian social policy has broken new ground by extending conditions to the spending of payments and using Indigenous peoples as trial participants. Australia and Aotearoa/New Zealand are the only countries to *compulsorily* quarantine a percentage of income support payments for approved expenses (Humpage, 2016: 552). While income management policies targeted at young benefit recipients in Aotearoa/New Zealand have not been explicitly framed as a Māori issue, the policies disproportionately impact Indigenous peoples in both countries (Humpage, 2016). Like Australia, Canada has explicitly targeted activation measures at First Nations recipients living on reserves. In 2013 Canada introduced the first pan-Canadian income support programme to make federal income support for First Nations people on reserves conditional on 'skills development and employment readiness' measures (Papillon, 2015: 9). First Nations recipients on reserves are the only Canadians to receive federal social assistance (Papillon, 2015: 1).

Concern about Indigenous welfare dependency is a common feature across the settler-colonies of Australia, Aotearoa/New Zealand and Canada. Debate about Māori 'misspending' of welfare has a long history. While Māori have always been officially eligible for the same entitlements as non-Māori, in practice, they were often paid lower benefits because of their supposed lower standard of living. Debate about Māori 'misspending' remained even after Māori political pressure ended the possibility of formal discrimination in 1945 (Humpage, 2010: 547). Scrutinising ideas of welfare dependency in Canada, Amber Gazso and colleagues (2020: 588) suggest that 'welfare dependency rhetoric has less visibly interacted with race in Canada'. However, survey data shows respondents still refer to welfare dependency to justify their view that Indigenous peoples unfairly access social assistance.

The racial politics of welfare is also shaped by local conditions and frameworks for settler–Indigenous–new migrant relations. In Aotearoa/New Zealand, a larger population of Māori share a common language and span a smaller land mass than in Australia. The emergence of an official policy of biculturalism in the 1980s, which established the 1840 Treaty of Waitangi as a model of governance, has informed welfare and multicultural policy. Biculturalism coincided with neoliberal reform that contracted out the delivery of government-funded social services to Māori organisations (Humpage, 2010: 550). Some Māori have critiqued biculturalism for ignoring Māori access to services and resources (Smits, 2011: 98). In the context of growing Asian migration since the 1990s, some Māori scholars and politicians framed official multiculturalism as an infringement on the particular claims of the Māori (Lowe, 2015). However, appeals to social justice and cultural diversity used to justify biculturalism have also been raised in defence of multiculturalism by the Labour government in office between 1999 and 2008 and the subsequent National government (Smits, 2011: 99).

Mean welfare has taken root and taken shape in different national, institutional and jurisdictional contexts. The deeply situated empirical focus of this book is given broader relevance by relating the details of the time, place and people that my research foregrounds to key concepts, such as access, vulnerability, shame and agency. These concepts have resonance across predominantly English-speaking, low-spending and targeted welfare states grappling with the legacies of colonialism, whether as metropole or colony, and accelerated migration.

3

Seatbelts and safety nets

Sabha got far more worked up by the topic of incivility than welfare entitlements, acknowledging the Parenting Payment (PP) (partnered) and Family Tax Benefit (FTB) she received with complacent pragmatism. The mother of three had lived in Australia for the last 15 years after migrating to marry her Pakistani-Australian husband. Family benefits supplemented earnings from her husband's work as a security guard. Like most of the people I interviewed, she named following the rules as the main obligation of citizenship: 'I think follow the rules and everything comes in rules, the traffic lights and when you go to the bank you need to make a queue, this kind of small things make a big difference. If you did these things you feel good and your country will be much beautiful.'

Sabha compared Australia with Pakistan, where she had grown up:

'Like, we don't wear seat belts [in Pakistan]. Yeah, mostly the traffics, when you get to the intersection here or to the roundabout, you have to wait for your turn, and in my country nobody waits, everybody wants to go as quick as he want to. These kinds of things. ... If you follow the rules our country has the potential, our people have the potential, if we follow the rules, we can come to [match] any civil country. Because we do have a lot of potential.'

For Sabha, following traffic rules and etiquette expressed mutual regard and the commitment to be civilised. But the orderliness of life in Australia was not the country's main drawcard for Sabha. She missed her family and wanted to return to Pakistan, but said she never would. Her husband had diabetes and healthcare and medicine was free here, in Australia, and expensive in Pakistan. Her children's schooling and future was here, and she wanted to stay with them. The *care about* others expressed through public order and the *care for* others provided through the welfare state for Sabha symbolised Australia's status as a civilised country.

Listening to Sabha talk about the importance of giving way at the intersection brought to mind Ghassan Hage's (2003) fable in the final chapter of his book, *Against Paranoid Nationalism*. Hage tells the story of Ali, a Lebanese man who arrived in Australia traumatised by the civil war. His loss and dislocation sent him mad and, in his madness, he was drawn to pedestrian crossings because they made him feel special. He would spend hours lingering at the crossing, revelling in the fact the traffic stopped for him. Ali's family joked that he refused to return to Lebanon with them because he would not leave behind the crossings. But Ali said he refused to return because Australia took care of him during his mental illness. Hage uses Ali's experience of the pedestrian crossing alongside theories of gift exchange to illustrate the difference between a contractual and an ethical model of mutual obligation. The neoliberal version of mutual obligation reduces reciprocity to a contractual exchange. Its proponents 'see it as unthinkable that the existing national culture should *yield* before the marginalised forms of social inhabitance they constantly encounter' (Hage, 2003: 147, emphasis in original). Genuine mutual obligation, in contrast, involves honouring the mere presence of others and the humanity it brings. Hage understands the crossing as a 'social gift' that structurally embeds the commitment to communal life; 'a space where people can enact a ritual of stopping and crossing, and through which society affirms itself as civilised (that is, ethical)' (147).

Of course, Hage uses this fable to make a case for the *ideal* of ethical reciprocity as the foundation of social care rather than an empirical claim about how things are. But this fable is striking for two reasons relevant to this chapter. First, it conjures an association between public order, on the one hand, and access to concrete social support, on the other, as related expressions of *care about* and *care for* members of a civilised society, which was echoed by some of the people I interviewed. Second, on a theoretical level, Hage's account of Ali feeling valued as the traffic yields for him and supported in his mental illness draws attention to the infrastructures, and everyday experiences of them, that give life to different ideas about social obligation and make certain forms of belonging possible. He does this in a way that foregrounds the role of the nation-state in creating the conditions that distribute a defensive or hopeful way of relating to others in society.

Hage's fable strikes a chord with theoretical approaches that foreground the 'social' dimension of social citizenship (Isin et al, 2008; Dean, 2013). This approach understands citizenship as more than a legal status that carries rights and duties. Citizenship includes the social lives and social relations through which 'we develop a sense of our rights as others' obligations and others' rights as our obligations' (Isin et al, 2008: 7). If social citizenship is fundamentally about the boundaries and terms of inclusion and exclusion in the citizenry (Patrick, 2017b: 294), this approach focuses on how those boundaries and terms are brought to life.

In this vein, this chapter considers how the people I interviewed framed their expectations of welfare provision, and how these expectations were negotiated and confirmed in the context of everyday experiences and biographical circumstances (Dwyer, 2000: 192; Dean, 2013: 11). I asked the people I interviewed questions about what makes a good citizen, whether they felt supported by the government, who should get help from the government and what kind of help they should receive. The first section is mainly descriptive, painting a broad outline of how the people I spoke to viewed welfare and citizenship. I only interviewed a small number of people, so this outline doesn't reveal anything about the extent or spread of support for welfare. But the diversity and complexity of the views expressed in interviews was consistent with the findings of larger studies of social security recipients (Murphy et al, 2011) and the Australian public (Wilson et al, 2009). And they contradicted popular claims that welfare recipients in particular (Saunders, 2004), and Australians in general (Tingle, 2012), have insatiable expectations of government support. The second section zooms in on individual stories to offer a thicker account of the forms of reciprocity people called on to claim and justify entitlement to social support and the different forms of belonging they signalled. I show the elastic ways people fit the details of their lives into normative ideas about duty and entitlement. Drawing on Hage, I think about social citizenship in terms of the social gift – be it well given or begrudgingly bestowed. Thinking about social welfare in this way draws attention to the material and emotional relations that produce and reproduce differentiated State–citizen relationships.

Support for welfare

Benefits based on need

Most of the people I spoke to said that those who need it should get government support, with basic need forming the basis of an implied collective right. This is in keeping with Australia's targeted welfare model of doing the most for the least well off, and is consistent with the preferences of the broader Australian public (Wilson et al, 2009). Still, collective services like public health and education were frequently named when I asked what tax revenue should be spent on and what form government support should take. Leena, a Lebanese-Australian mother living on PP and her husband's income, put it this way: 'Don't give us money, give the places we need to go – schools and hospitals.'

Speaking generally, the elderly and people incapacitated by illness or difficult circumstances were considered first in line for government support. More personally, many counted themselves among those in need, particularly as parents or families struggling with the cost of living. Reem, a Lebanese-Australian single mother of three children living on PP (single), started crying as she answered, 'People that really need it [should get help from the government]. People like myself who have struggled with health and with you know, no family to help me take care of the kids'. Tracey, an Aboriginal mother of a large family, likewise said, 'People who are really in need ... homeless, very, very low-income earners ... people with illnesses'.

When I asked whether she would put herself in that category, she replied, 'Yes I would, definitely'. Reem and Tracey's own experience of disadvantage confirmed the need for state provision.

Stereotypes about welfare recipients choosing an easy life on welfare loomed large for some, who defended their right to support by insisting on their genuine need:

'Like, for example, I tell you my own situation, I am getting benefits, but still I can't make much out of that, I still have to suffer from many problems and we still have to make many sacrifices, it is not that the government is supporting and we are just like living a very good life and we are just enjoying, it's nothing like that, we're just getting a very small amount, so the government should improve there.' (Nadira, Pakistani mother of two, recent skilled migrant receiving FTB)

'I do receive money from Centrelink but I don't feel comfortable. It's not like I'm receiving this money and I'm, you know, I'm enjoying it because I'm not, it's just going towards our needs.' (Reem, Lebanese-Australian single mother of three children living on the single Parenting Payment)

'Some people also are making fun [saying] people just want handouts. Some making fun; the ones that don't have families and the ones that don't have kids think it's a joke. It's not like we're making the money, raking it in, living the luxury life and driving a Mercedes Benz, it's nothing like that. Just need a little help that's all.' (Aisha, Lebanese-Australian mother of two, husband's earnings supplemented by family benefits)

Aisha's defensiveness was heightened by the rhetoric around proposed cuts to spending in the 2014 Federal Budget, with Treasurer Hockey (2014) insisting there should be 'more household income coming from personal effort than from the government'. She resented the idea that families should make more effort to tighten their belt:

'We are already tightening our belt! Don't speak for us ... there's a reason why we got it in the first place, because obviously it's not manageable with life being so expensive. Nothing's cheap. Homes are not cheap. Homes are the most expensive compared to anywhere else in the world.'

The rhetoric of personal effort and belt tightening made a mockery of the reality of going without to make ends meet.

Despite these complaints, the majority of the people I spoke to said that they felt supported by the government. Those who didn't tended to associate the government with politicians they distrusted. Kane, a young Aboriginal man with no source of income after quitting the unemployment benefit said emphatically, 'I don't feel no support'. Nessa, also Aboriginal, and a single mother on PP (single) added, 'We feel no love from 'em [the politicians]'. But many others, even those who complained about the government, said they felt supported, usually citing their welfare payments and family benefits, but sometimes the wider range of public services and infrastructure in Australia. The idea that Australians were more fortunate than those in other countries recurred, usually compared to the countries their families had migrated from or the generic 'third world'. For example, Leena said 'I tell my husband I kiss the ground of Australia, we are so lucky, we can bitch and moan as much as we want, we are so lucky', describing the conditions in Lebanon when she visited with her Lebanese husband. However, her sister expressed the sense that the collective benefits Australians enjoy were under threat by the proposed budget, 'We're a pretty lucky country but I mean if Abbott [prime minister at the time] comes in and changes these changes there's going to be a lot more [people struggling]'.

Conditional benefits

While the idea that 'anyone that needs it' should get help from the government recurred, for many it was tempered by concern about undeserving beneficiaries and unfair distribution. Many of the same people who advocated government responsibility for helping those in need and creating more inclusive social services also endorsed some form of conditions attached to welfare payments. Conditional welfare was usually justified in terms of curbing destructive behaviour, promoting a work ethic or making sure people don't 'get something for nothing'. Jasmin, a mother of two originally from Hong Kong who worked part time and received PP (single), assumed that many welfare recipients were not legitimately in need but just lazy, 'So push them into work or study instead of sitting at home'. She was among those who highlighted individual causes of poverty and was convinced that it was necessary to change the behaviour of people receiving welfare. But even those who emphasised individual causes of poverty tended to say the government should be responsible for looking after the poor to stop social breakdown. As Jasmin put it, 'If you don't help them there'll be more problems, they'll be on the street'.

Support for conditional welfare was more often qualified. For example, Christina, a Chinese-born mother of two receiving family benefits, thought that job search conditions and sanctions should be attached to benefits to encourage the unemployed to look for work, but she was also concerned about barriers to employment like racism. Bill, an older Aboriginal man on the Age Pension, thought the unemployed should be made to do community work or study to prepare them for employment, but he was also conscious that there was a lack of work. Nessa didn't object to conditional welfare in principle, only its blanket application, which tarnished her as dysfunctional. 'They [welfare agencies] just keep watching ya and you had to go to playgroup to keep your house', she told me bitterly. She suggested it was appropriate for some others but not her, adding that 'the girls in there [the compulsory playgroup], they actually do need help'. Those who spoke in favour of conditional welfare often took this stance. They were in favour of conditional measures as long as their implementation accounted for individual circumstances, especially those outside people's control. Such partial and qualified support for conditional welfare is common in studies of welfare users' perspectives (see, for example, Dwyer, 2000; Murphy et al, 2011).

Ideas about the relationship between citizenship rights and obligations were reflected in views about who should get support from the government and descriptions of what makes a 'good citizen'. Many of the people I spoke to named paid work as the main characteristic of a good citizen because it contributes to individual and collective welfare, either through payment of taxes or fostering a strong economy. As Jasmin put it, 'work to help themselves and the country'. Samah's description of a good citizen as 'someone that puts something back as well as gets back' foregrounded the importance of contribution. This idea was echoed in her view that 'people that have worked a little bit' should get assistance from the government. While Samah implied that contribution was part of the bargain individuals made in return for certain benefits, her sister Leena suggested a more collective vision of contribution as pulling together for everyone's benefit (see Dean, 2013). 'Help support the country, that's how it should be', she added to her sister's input.

Forms of contributing other than paid work tended to be raised more as an ideal than a concrete obligation of citizenship. Jasmin distinguished between a good citizen and a good community member: 'If it's a good citizen it's just like don't do anything illegal but the community you need to do activities and all these kinds of things. ... Part of the community means you say you join them and try to help and organise things. That's called part of the community.' Good citizens follow the rules, but good community members are active and involved outside of their private lives. Following the rules was the most common citizenship obligation identified by the people I interviewed, sometimes narrowly defined as obeying the law, and other times more broadly as being civil and respectful to others. When I asked Jasmin if she was part of a community according to her definition, she said, 'No I don't think so. I'm just the audience or something'. Jane, an Anglo mother of two, like Jasmin, lived on a part-time income supplemented by the parenting payment. She said a good local citizen follows the rules – 'I'm always told I'm a goodie-goodie' – and a great one helps out. The idea that active civic participation went beyond the minimum obligations of citizenship was common. Contributing through paid work, on the other hand, was more often painted as a non-negotiable citizenship obligation.

Reducing contribution to paid work casts people who are reliant on welfare payments as having failed in their obligations and owing a citizenship debt (Dwyer, 2004: 268). T.S. Marshall (1977) defined the social rights of citizenship as the guarantee of a minimum standard of living and the benefit of participation in society. Conditionality insists that these guarantees depend on meeting citizenship responsibilities, ranging from 'a general duty to make a recognised contribution to wider society' to 'specified tasks or forms of behaviour' tied to accessing specific benefits (Dwyer, 2000: 205). The idea that welfare recipients 'shouldn't get something for nothing' implies unfairness, a theme that is often at the heart of welfare debates and recurred in interviews. Expressions of unfairness say a lot about a sense of obligation and belonging to society and the country.

Unfairness

Monica, who was among the most vocal supporters of conditional welfare, was unique for insisting she personally should be subjected to harsher welfare rules. She self-critically reflected, 'How do you say to a person who works every day of their life and pays tax that someone else deserves not to work and still get paid? Why is that fair? That man working over there has to pay for my dinner. How do I tell him that anyway?' Monica echoed the reprimand delivered with the 2014 Federal Budget: 'We must always remember that when a person receives an entitlement from the government, in comes from the pocket of another person' (Hockey, 2014). If citizenship was a give-and-take contract among bargaining individuals, as conditionality implied, then she was taking from the pockets of her hardworking fellow citizens.

Others pointed to the unfairness of other people who were less deserving than them benefiting from welfare. This usually surfaced as resentment about people 'rorting the system', many claiming they knew people or knew *of* people taking advantage of the system. I often found it difficult to distinguish personal experience from general gossip when people complained about welfare cheats. A few told me they knew people rorted the system because they saw it on the television. Rorting was used to describe people lying and claiming more than they should, not spending their payments appropriately, or not genuinely looking for work. Young people, single mothers and the unemployed – among the most stigmatised groups in public portrayals of permissive welfare – were most of often named as claiming payments they don't really need at the expense of others. When support is reserved for the most in need, people jostle for the classification of 'genuinely needy'. Unfairness was expressed by some as a personal grievance about not being eligible for certain benefits or having no alternative but to rely on social security. As Tracey said, 'Very upsetting, especially for the ones who don't have anything and sort of have no choice but be on a Centrelink payment really'.

While it wasn't unusual for those I interviewed to look sideways for examples of unfairness, many also pointed to their unfair treatment at the hands of the government or the general unfairness of social inequality. As Leena said, 'the rich stay rich, the poor stay poor', and her sister echoed 'I think it needs to be brought together more – the rich and poor shouldn't be that fat line in between'. Kane defiantly described receiving welfare as 'getting one back off the government'. Entitlement to a 'hand up' was in these cases framed as a matter of fairness.

The hypocrisy of focusing on the behaviour – especially spending habits – of welfare recipients recurred among interviewees alive to systemic unfairness. While complaining about people wasting payments on gambling, Samah shifted gear and added, 'But in saying that why are you [government] not taking away pokie machines, because they make too much money, that's another disrespectful thing'. For Kane, Nessa and Luke, three Aboriginal young adults, income management was the perfect example of systemic discrimination and control of Aboriginal people in the name of welfare. It started as a race-based measure only targeting Aboriginal people in remote communities of the Northern Territory, restricting where and on what they could spend their social security payments. As Nessa said bitterly, 'What? Cos you're working you're entitled to a drink and smoke? That's unfair. That really is unfair'.

Speaking to me not long after the 2014 Federal Budget announcement, some people were particularly sensitive to the hypocrisy of politicians and government. Ronda, an Aboriginal mother whose husband's income was supplemented by her PP, was incredulous at the gall of politicians who live on tax revenue and shape society through their policies but who vilify welfare recipients:

> 'For Tony Abbott to say "if you can't afford it don't have it" – we had it before you hiked everything up, so you're making it worse for us. They're happy, they have multimillion dollar homes, they have people that chauffer them around. They don't have to pay for petrol, they don't have to wait in lines, they get everything done for them.'

She implied that the government was breaking its agreement to be there for citizens by 'just taking, taking, taking'. Leena also blamed the government for creating the difficult circumstances that made welfare necessary: 'They've killed the jobs, they've sold everything off to overseas ... so where's the jobs for people – and then he [former prime minister Tony Abbott] said get off the dole you bludgers. Well where is the work? You're creating these people, they go well just keep us on the dole, there's no work.' Their incredulity expressed the expectation that the government should rightfully cushion people from the effects of external pressures such as the cost of living and lessen, not create, social inequalities.

Through the question of who should get support from the government, the boundaries of national membership are drawn. Leena insisted that Australians should get support from the government, particularly Australian companies that create jobs – 'help the people that help Australia'. Ronda emphasised collective responsibility above individual contribution, but nonetheless hinged on national belonging:

> 'People in our own backyard [should get help from the government]. Money needs to stay here. You know, we are the multicultural country of the world – we need to support our young people, our old people. If they don't have support from the government and families are working that hard just to pay their own bills, no one's gonna look after them.'

While Ronda was careful to include multicultural Australians in her vision of the nation, Bill viewed claimants 'from different countries' as 'ripping the money off people that need the money'. He described the queue at Centrelink as 'the whole lot of them from different countries'. The implication was that they were visibly not Australian and therefore not genuinely entitled to welfare. Bill also rejected the idea that Aboriginal people like himself were owed a debt because of what they have lost and suffered through colonisation, repeatedly disparaging what he described as 'a typical blackfella, always "they owe me"'.

National belonging was repeatedly called on to claim entitlement, although how national belonging was defined varied and shifted – a point I take up in the following section. Among the small and diverse group of people I interviewed, their shared views and expectations of welfare cut across ethno-cultural background. But Aboriginal interviewees and those from non-English-speaking migrant backgrounds sometimes referred explicitly to cultural difference to explain their expectations and feelings of entitlement in a way that Anglo interviewees did not. For example, Jasmin explained her complacent pragmatism about welfare, by saying: 'I come from Hong Kong. They [the government] don't give you anything so I think it's right, they shouldn't give you anything. If they give you [support] it's a bonus but if they don't give you that's life. That's where I come from so that's what I think about that.' Bill repeatedly characterised fellow Aboriginal people as work-averse and over-entitled (echoing familiar stereotypes), 'As I said the black fella he's too lazy to get out and work because he thinks the world owes him something'. In contrast, Kane defiantly described receiving welfare as 'getting one back off the government' that tried to keep Aboriginal people down. Cardona and her colleagues similarly found that carers from culturally and linguistically diverse backgrounds expressed ideas about not wanting to ask for too much or be a burden on the system. Their feelings about accessing entitlements were influenced by migration history, sometimes expressed as a conflicting sense of gratitude and fear of drawing attention to themselves (Cardona et al, 2006: 54). The following section further situates welfare claims in the details of experience and biography by turning to a more fine-grained picture of individual stories.

The spirit of the gift

The principle of reciprocity is at the heart of gift exchange. Hage imagines the pedestrian crossing as an ethical 'social gift' because it offers everyone recognition in return for simply being. But gifts aren't necessarily positive. They can be affirming or undermining, fuelled by motives that 'range from love and sympathy to insecurity and anxiety, to power and prestige, to self-interest and overt hostility' (Komter, 2005: 54). Thinking of social welfare as a gift foregrounds the spirit in which it is given and the relationships it makes possible. Welfare regimes institutionalise reciprocity based on an implicit social contract that names expectations and obligations not only among citizens and between them and their governments, but also between family members whose caring obligations and relationships are shaped by welfare arrangements (Komter, 2005: 146). There are multiple and competing versions of reciprocity embedded in welfare arrangements, as Chapter 4 shows at the street level of community service provision. Welfare users invoke various forms of reciprocity in their talk about welfare, and by doing so position themselves in relation to the nation and its resources, and their claims on them.

Nadira

Nadira was in her late 20s and trying to find stable footing in a new country after moving from Pakistan with her husband and two children on a permanent skilled visa. She had newly enrolled in a PhD programme on a modest scholarship. Nadira had an expansive view of what welfare was, describing not only cash payments but also the family support programmes offered by the local council (where we met) and public services such as libraries: 'I often go to the library. There's a preschool programme for children over there and I come to this family hub, so it's very good, my children get a lot of benefits because they get to interact with other people and gain confidence through the activities.' Local services were important entry point into public life in a new country, which Nadira had actively sought out by searching the internet. And they provided a place to take the children without spending money – a welcome outlet, because the family was struggling to find skilled work and meet the high cost of living in Australia.

When I met Nadira, there was a waiting period of two years before most newly arrived migrants could access most welfare payments and concessions, except family assistance payments. By the time of writing, the federal government had doubled the waiting period to four years. Nadira was grateful for the Family Tax Benefit (FTB) and public services she could access, but she was disappointed that she was not eligible for more financial support at the time when she needed it most: 'I don't know why it's that they support more after two years – I just have this in my mind that it would have been better if they would have supported when somebody is new over here rather than when he's old and he's good enough to bear everything himself.'

Nadira saw government provision for skilled migrants who had borne the emotional and financial cost of migrating as inadequate. She considered it part of the government's responsibility to create the opportunities for work and support those who couldn't find work:

'I don't know why the Australian government is inviting so many migrants from other parts of the world since there are not enough jobs ... if they need skilled migrants they should also create opportunities for them if they want somebody to leave their house and everything from another country and they are coming here and they're not getting a job, then it would be very bad because somebody leaves everything.'

The implied economic contract between her and the government was clearly defined through the terms of her migration on a skilled visa. Nadira spoke many times about her relationship with the Australian government as a kind of mutual investment: 'I want to serve Australia with my skills', 'the government has invested on me and it is my duty I should do something for them' and later, 'if I am getting any payment and they are investing on me, I should also give the best out of me'. She expected to contribute to the country by working and to be given the opportunity to do so.

Dina

Dina was a mother in her early 30s, born in Australia to Lebanese parents and married to a Lebanese man she had met in Lebanon. Her husband worked while she looked after their two young children, for which she received PP. They weren't struggling, but their mortgage and the unexpected cost of medical bills for family back in Lebanon absorbed much of their income. Dina described the PP she received as recognition of her care work as a parent. When I asked her how she felt about receiving the benefit, she reflected:

> 'I feel good because – I mean, look, something just came to mind now. I've never thought about it before but it feels nice to also be recognised that when you are at home raising your children that you are actually being recognised as doing something important and that you might need – so it's nice to be able to know that while you are doing the most important job in the world, that financially, you don't have to be worried. You don't have to choose between leaving your kids with other people to be raised or to be financially stable.'

She implied that it was a gift to be able to stay at home and raise her children without financial strain, but also that she was contributing something important and necessary. This strikes a chord with the idea of parenting as informal work with a public benefit. Her husband's paid work shielded Dina from the gendered stigma associated with single mothers on income support. The pre-employment mutual obligation programme, ParentsNext, which targets younger parents and parents who are long-term welfare recipients, had not yet been introduced (Klein, 2021).

Dina told me she was disappointed that her payment was reduced as her husband earned more, which she described as stifling their personal effort to 'try to do better': 'He is out there working and trying to do what he has to do and sometimes through his work and what he gets, we get much less. I would hope that wouldn't be the case.' But she mainly expressed gratitude for the gift of being supported to raise her children, and for the security and comfort the welfare system gave her, both in previous tough times and in case of unanticipated future need:

> 'It's been a blessing to be able to – when times have been tough and when my husband has been between jobs, just to know that you have that support. I can't even imagine being in a situation like my in-laws in Lebanon where they don't have much money and they don't have support from the hospitals and so forth.
>
> What I do know from other people in my family is that there are different types of Parenting Payments. So depending on your situation, you can get more. So, for example, if you have a child with a special need and you are taking care of them, you can actually get more. So depending on – maybe if I was ever in a situation where I needed more or something happened, that gives me comfort to know that there are different levels of payment if I ever needed to access them.'

The comparative experience of her family in Lebanon highlighted the benefits she received in Australia. The security Dina described conjured a sense of citizenship as a form of solidarity that provides collective protection against shared risks. Like Ali in Hage's fable, she felt recognised and cared for, and her resulting security confirmed her belonging and faith in the national collective.

Monica

Dina's feeling of recognition for her caring work stood in sharp contrast to Monica's intense shame as a single, non-working parent (discussed further in Chapter 5). Monica dismissed the idea that raising her child was an adequate contribution given she wasn't working to financially support herself or her family. An Anglo mother, also in her early 30s, she had relied on welfare payments as her only source of income since she left home as a teenager. She was one of the few examples of unqualified support for conditional welfare among the people I spoke to, and she also stood out for including herself among those who needed stricter compliance with welfare rules: 'Anybody who needs it [should get help from the government] for a specific amount of time with regulations.' She repeatedly described the social security system and mutual obligations attached to payments as 'too easy', enabling people to sit around while others had to work. Her own self-destructive drug habit and the destructive behaviour of people around her, including her siblings whom she was forced to care for from a young age, convinced her of the logic of paternalism: 'It needs to be like America maybe, six weeks and you're kicked off. Because what choice would I have, I'm not going to let my kid starve, I would get a job. I would have to get a job.'

Monica was the most insistent that relying on welfare payments amounted to failed responsibility to provide for oneself and family or contribute to collective welfare. When I asked her how society in general treats people on welfare, she replied:

'Like they should mostly, and I'm one of them, and I don't think that – like they don't contribute, I suppose. Maybe sometimes it's unfair, people look down at people and I think in a way it's cementing their position in welfare by looking down on them because they're never going to feel worthy of being anything else if society says you're crap because you take money off the government. But at the same time they are doing that, they are taking money off the government when they could have a job. So I don't know, probably pretty fairly I think, which is mean. Like, it's harsh, but we're spoilt.'

While Monica acknowledged the way that stigmatising people on welfare undermined their self-worth and motivation, she concluded that the judgement was fair because they, like her, lacked the virtues of self-responsibility and self-reliance. She offered up her shame as her only way to pay the symbolic debt she had incurred. Monica had accepted and absorbed the 'mean' and grudging spirit with which welfare is given to single parents and the unemployed, judging herself as harshly as she felt others judged her.

Mick

Mick was a father whose work as a handyman was supplemented by his partner's family benefits. He was a proud Aboriginal man who described himself as self-reliant – 'I've got my own business so I pretty much look after myself' – but appreciated the benefit he received from tax breaks and public infrastructure. Mick considered Australians lucky, but not spoilt. He described a documentary he had seen where an English garbage man employed by the council worked collecting garbage in 'an Asian country 12 hours a day, 7 days a week', and insisted, 'The roads, all the infrastructure, people just don't understand how lucky we are in Australia'. Mick stood out for his unconditionally generous and optimistic outlook: 'Anyone what [sic] needs it really [should get help from the government]. We're a first class country. We've got the infrastructure to help people.' His view that 'the rest of the country [should look after poor people], like with tax and that' suggested the sense of solidarity also evoked by Dina. Mick foregrounded poverty as circumstance rather than choice – what he called people's 'back story' – and he strongly rejected moral judgements about people's situation and behaviour, saying, 'I think it's disgusting and low that you can judge someone without knowing anything about them'.

While Mick compared Australia's fortunes with other countries, another point of reference was his grandparents' experience of having their lives utterly controlled by welfare authorities, which he compared to his own situation living in Aboriginal housing with opportunities 'wide open' to him:

'But they weren't allowed to own their own home. They had to move o'n to a mission where there was a mission manager; his job was to look after Aboriginal people, allegedly. But he walked around – could walk into anyone's house when he wanted to make sure the house was clean and what not. So they couldn't buy a house; they couldn't leave an inheritance to my parents ... now I'm in a situation where, the third generation down the line where I'm able enough to save, start saving money to hopefully one day purchase a house.'

He echoed the commonly expressed view of a good citizen – 'pay my taxes and keep out of trouble' – although for Mick and a few others the obligation to follow the rules touched an emotional nerve: 'Bad behaviour, I'm not a big fan of bad behaviour. I think everyone should act civilised, at least civilised to each other. You don't have to be nice but you don't have to be a jerk.' The importance of obeying the law had an added significance for Mick as an Aboriginal man alive to the threat of police harassment and the reality of Aboriginal incarceration in a country where Aboriginal people make up 3 per cent of the population but 27 per cent of prisoners (Rattan and Mountain, 2016). He repeated his father's advice to him: 'Don't give the police any reason to talk to you', adding, 'that great bit of advice from my dad has kept me out of trouble my whole life.'

Mick's idea of a good local citizen was someone who looked beyond their personal and familial life – 'Someone who will take time out of their day' and 'sacrifice time from their own families to help out other people'. He saw his role in his Aboriginal community as brokering support, describing how he made inquiries on behalf of other Aboriginal fathers who 'get shame' in the face of welfare service providers. He called this his 'little personal obligation', a skill he was equipped for by being one of the elder siblings in an Aboriginal family with the responsibility to 'look after everyone else'.

Christina

Christina was a Chinese-Australian mother of two in her late 20s receiving PP. Her husband worked as a labourer and they lived in a granny flat at the back of her parents' house. When we first spoke one child was living with her and the other was being cared for by her grandmother in China, who was waiting for a visa to come to Australia. Christina insisted that welfare spending should prioritise parents, especially pregnant women, because 'pregnant lady is two lives in one'. Like Mick, being respectful and following the rules was at the heart of her idea of citizenship obligations. Her version of a good citizen also emphasised order, but was more privately oriented: 'Try not to get in a mess. You are responsible for your own property, for the grass outside [the nature strip alongside public footpaths], for your bin.' Christina named these duties as part of the social contract that protected her freedoms and rewarded her with benefits: 'In Australia I have a right to do what I want, just don't break the rules. If we follow the rules, the government should reward us.'

Contrasting Australia with China was key to Christina's positioning of herself as *part of* the nation, and not just in terms of formal citizenship status and benefits. She got worked up about what she saw as uncivil behaviour, bringing up the difference between Australia and China to make her point.

In China, she said, people won't give up their seat on the bus or train to a woman with a child:

> 'In Australia people are more polite, in China not really. And it's like they don't care if you've got a child or not in China, if you're on transport. But here, they care about you, they care about the child. They offer you whatever they can. If they're on a bus and they're sitting on a seat and there's no other seat they offer you their seat. In China – no – that's it. My seat is my seat until I get off.'

Like Sabha, Christina described courteous and civil behaviour as a sign of *caring about* strangers in public. She continued, by pointing to Australia's public *care for* citizens:

> 'Also, Chinese hospitals you gotta line up, pay money, just to see a doctor. After you see a doctor you gotta pay for your, um, medication. But *here* when you see a doctor you don't have to pay money. You just give them your card, if you're Australian citizen. If you're not, then you have to pay money.'

Christina could have been simply listing the differences between the two countries and what she saw as the benefits of living in Australia, from its orderly public etiquette to its welfare system. But she also seemed to *associate* those benefits with her construction of Australia as a civilised country and herself as part of it.

Christina, like Sabha, implied that following the rules – whether those implied in etiquette or formalised in law – is not just a formal requirement but also an expression of emotional investment in the nation. As 'an indicator of how much one "cares"', emotional investment is a form of participation in society that Hage calls 'participatory belonging' (2001: 334). Despite formally being an Australian citizen, Sabha felt unqualified to comment on the desirable traits of Australian citizens except through comparison with Pakistan: 'It's really hard for me because I am not Australian; I'm Pakistani, so this one is hard for me.' Christina, on the other hand, asserted her judgement as an explicit marker of her 'Australianness': 'They [people in China] should learn from Australian people: be kind, be responsible, and be polite. If they can do all these three things, when they come to our country we'll do exactly the same.' Christina's decisiveness, in contrast to Sabiha's hesitancy, perhaps expressed an entitlement to make judgements about the management of the nation. Hage (1998: 45–6) identifies this as 'governmental belonging', which he sees as distinct from a more 'passive' mode of belonging expressed in the expectation to simply to 'be part of' and 'benefit from' the nation.

Conclusion

The responses of the small but diverse range of people I interviewed suggest more about dynamics than patterns of expectation. While people drew on popularly endorsed ideas about entitlement and duty, these normative scripts were loaded with references to their own personal biography and social circumstances. Daniel Edmiston (2018) also shows how material circumstances informed lay accounts of social citizenship among deprived and affluent citizens in the UK. He argues that lived experiences of deprivation make poor people more attuned to the external factors that affect their capacity to shape the world and their unequal position in it (Edmiston, 2018: 69).

The examples I have foregrounded suggest that people fit the details of everyday life into the normative scripts they evoke to claim and defend their social rights. Nadira invoked an economic form of reciprocity as 'mutual investment' befitting her reception to Australia as a skilled migrant; she regarded the Australian government as having reneged on its side of the contract to provide the conditions that enable her ability to productively participate and be self-sufficient. Dina's views of welfare were inflected by her experience as a stay-at-home mother with a working husband – she felt valued and recognised for her work as a parent and comforted by the safety net the welfare state provided. In contrast, Monica's care work as a single parent could not assuage the acute shame of not providing financially for herself or her daughter; she endorsed the punitive nature of much conditional welfare and absorbed the moral authoritarian judgements it relies on. Mick's inclusive view of welfare implied the collective responsibility to ensure wellbeing, his optimism in part informed by the opportunities open to him in comparison with the previous generations of his Aboriginal family. Christina and Sabha described behaving in a civil manner as not simply an obligation of citizenship but also an embodiment of civic care and potential, brought into relief by their comparison of Australia with the countries they had migrated from.

Despite the diverse ways of approaching and receiving social support that these examples show, they are underpinned by the structural fact of welfare and citizenship apparatuses that make different ways of relating to social welfare possible. Thinking about social welfare in terms of gift exchange does not imply, as some conservative critics of the welfare state might, that welfare should be taken as a gift rather than a right or entitlement. Instead, Hage's emphasis on the spirit of the gift helps refine our understanding of the nature of inequality embedded in the institutional arrangements of the welfare state. He insists that belonging and exclusion are not only dependent on formal eligibility, but also on the mode of access to citizenship. Hage argues, 'Where the problem of inequality and discrimination emerge is not around questions of accessing rights as much as it is in the *mode* of accessing such rights' (2002: 4; original emphasis). Here he emphasises the difference between a 'dishonouring mode of delivering services' that is demeaning and one that preserves dignity and gives rise to what he calls 'honourable citizenship'. This thinking foreshadows the ideal of the ethical spirit embodied in the social gift that he develops in *Against Paranoid Nationalism* (2003).

Of course, the denial of rights, including welfare rights, to those excluded from formal citizenship has real and dire consequences (Dwyer and Brown, 2005; McKay and Dunn, 2015). But drawing attention to the *mode* of accessing rights helps understand the problem of inequality and discrimination for those who are formally, although sometimes only partially, included. Certain sub-groups – including migrants, Indigenous people, single parents and the unemployed – may be formally included as citizens but cast as incapable or underserving of existing citizenship. Whether the people I interviewed received welfare as a social gift defensively or graciously seemed to relate to the claimant category they fell into, combined with their family and work situation – whether they or their partner were also engaged in paid work. It also reflected where they located themselves in the divide between rich and poor, which they often related to personal and proximate injustices. The degree of defensiveness expressed by respondents is hardly surprising given the maligning spirit with which social security is extended to welfare recipients in general and certain categories of claimants in particular.

As I mentioned in Chapter 2, the combination of mean and lean welfare payments and government outsourcing of service provision draws welfare users increasingly into the orbit of charities and community organisations. Chapter 4 continues to explore modes of access at the street level of community welfare services. It shows how embodied interpretations of reciprocity inform judgements about the 'deserving vulnerability' and 'empowered responsibility' of welfare users coming into contact with community welfare services.

Problems of access in community welfare

'It's interesting, the second-generation Arabic-speaking group in the area; that's a very interesting group to work with and not necessarily easy', Janet offered in response to my question about whether there are some groups of service users that are more responsible than others. At first she referred vaguely to 'certain cultural groups' but, like most of the staff I had spoken to, was hesitant to elaborate.

Janet was one of the frontline staff I interviewed from the local community service sector. I asked Janet to explain her response and – as if given license – she continued at length:

'Because they often think they know everything, and they're confident, some of them, probably over-confident. They usually were born here, gone through Australian schools, primary schools, secondary school. And married young; have lots of children. And some people, some are quite loud, they talk, they do everything. They think they know a lot, but not necessarily so. And sometimes, actually, it's easier to work with newly arrived migrants, because they think they don't know. They know they don't know. They know they need to learn something; they are very happy to be helped, or to be introduced to a different system. While second-generation people often think they know everything; they know more.'

She suggested that the low 'participation rate' of second-generation Arabic speakers in welfare services was down to this self-assurance, a mistaken perception that 'they already know more'. Perhaps they don't need the services because they already have extensive social networks, she speculated, but then 'the results of the children's achievement' suggest otherwise.

Later, however, reflecting on the fairness of the welfare system, Janet suggested that second-generation Arabic speakers arrogantly expect rather than refuse support. She described being approached by a new migrant mother who was ineligible for a support programme. The woman had a young child and was unable to work due to an illness, but her husband worked. The woman complained that it was unfair that mothers who drive big, expensive, petrol-guzzling cars can access the programme when her family relies on one income for five people but was not eligible:

'And I thought, "Well, what can I say?" It's unfair, definitely. Because I've seen all those women, they've got the latest of fashion. They're mostly second-generation, Arabic-speaking. And also got a bit of racial tension because people thinking, "Those people". And there are few of them, they came as a big group, and people complain to me, they say, "They're arrogant". The reason they are arrogant is because they think they know everything; they speak English.'

Markers of Arab women's excess and undue entitlement reappeared in staff interviews as well as in the accounts of the Lebanese-Australian women I spoke to – the large cars, the ostentatious jewellery and adherence to fashion.

Janet's account of the incident exemplified the problem of access, which was a recurring theme in my conversations with community service staff and in the programmes I volunteered in as part of my research. Frontline staff defined access as both a primary goal and challenge of service delivery. My questions about the responsibilities of service staff and service users often elicited reflection on the challenges of reaching 'difficult-to-access' groups on the one hand, and curbing improper access of services on the other. Many programmes promoted access for disadvantaged or isolated individuals as initiating the process of empowerment, yet all operated within the constraints of limited resources and increasingly targeted provision.

The problem of access was animated by a tension between under-access and over-access – where accessing services could be figured as either a positive initiative to improve one's circumstances or negative opportunism that abuses the system. These characterisations of service access coloured how frontline staff interpreted and classified the need and entitlement of service users.

Second-generation Arabic speakers – specifically women – appeared as contradictory exemplars of the problem of access. Janet characterised them as arrogant because, on the one hand, they refused support, and on the other, they expected it. She read loudness, arriving in larger groups and speaking English as betraying their arrogance, implying wilful self-importance or entitlement and lack of gratitude. The contrast Janet drew between newly arrived migrants as receptive to help and second-generation migrants who 'think they know everything' drew on cultural narratives about the genuinely needy and deserving as receptive to, but not expectant of, support. This case illustrates how the problem of access is a site through which the enduring distinction between 'deserving' and 'undeserving' poor is renewed and reworked.

It is worth spelling out that the point of Janet's example and the problem it illustrates is not to expose the prejudice of community sector workers. Most of the workers I spoke to, Janet included, thoughtfully reflected on the complex causes of disadvantage and how the boundaries of entitlement were drawn. Many were reluctant to generalise about service users, especially in terms of cultural differences. They puzzled over how precisely culture mattered with fellow community workers, but were cautious to articulate it in a formal interview, in part because the answers seemed elusive, and partly because it might lead to the fraught territory of cultural stereotyping. The fear of stereotyping and simplifying culture meant that there was a common professional knowledge that culture mattered, but a reluctance to articulate how (resembling anxiety about essentialising culture in academia). A number of staff were uncomfortable speaking in these terms, and yet their responses suggested considerable prior reflection. Some even said that they were willing to voice the sense they had of how culture mattered to me because my research might help shed light on the issue.

The role of the community sector

A key characteristic of welfare reforms since the 1970s has been the escalating move away from direct State provision of social support and the growing responsibility of voluntary sector organisations for delivering services largely funded and regulated by the State. Reformers of various persuasions have presented 'community' as an ideal site for meeting social needs and shaping citizens in the name of ground-up and cost-efficient social support. Some view this transformation as the epitome of welfare state decline and the neoliberal offloading of responsibility and risk from the State to individuals, families and communities. But the various motives that drive community services suggest a more uneven and ambiguous shift, with neoliberal values of entrepreneurialism and competition coexisting with more supportive and caring impulses (DeVerteuil, 2015).

The community welfare organisations in the vicinity of my fieldwork specialised in resourcing the highly culturally and linguistically diverse profile of the area. Broadly speaking, welfare services were delivered by ethno or religious organisations with a welfare branch and generalist welfare organisations that were nonetheless tailored to the cultural and linguistic diversity of the local population. Community services aim to support families in their caring roles or step in when families are unable to provide care for children, older people or people with disabilities. Growing investment in family support services reflects the increasing emphasis on early intervention to improve child welfare by addressing problems before they become entrenched or escalate into crisis (Australian Institute of Family, 2015). Support services can include therapeutic care, developing parenting knowledge and skills, and promoting safe and supportive families and communities (Australian Institute of Health and Welfare, 2017: 3). I interviewed 11 staff from generalist welfare organisations, most of which housed an array of family support programmes and activities, clinical services and ethno-specific community groups, and ran primarily on funding from local, state and federal government grants. I also participated in and observed key initiatives and operational activities across a few organisations.

Access to Empower (positive access)

During my time spent with organisations, access was often expressed as the doorway to capacity- and community-building. The importance of making key services accessible to those most in need reflects 'social inclusion and cost-effectiveness' as key concerns in human service provision (Cortis, 2012: 351). It also reflects concerns that the intended beneficiaries of services targeted at those most in need can be the hardest to involve, particularly in early intervention and prevention programmes (Cortis et al, 2009: v). Embedding interventions targeting disadvantaged families in universal services or venues is a popular strategy for engaging 'hard-to-reach' individuals or groups (Cortis, 2012: 355).

The organisation I volunteered in facilitated a number of soft-entry activities in partnership with other community welfare organisations and the local council, through which I met an interagency network of frontline staff. As the name suggests, soft-entry programmes aim to draw participants into contact with services through indirect and unintimidating activities such as playgroups, excursions and arts and crafts. As one worker described, 'it's based around fun stuff ... it isn't intensive and it's not going to freak them out'. They serve to hook people in so they can be referred on to need-specific services as well as building informal networks with other participants.

Staff examples of success stories often reflected the goal of connecting people to services and community. For example, Lihn described a case of an isolated Vietnamese mother with post-natal depression. The mother never left the house and she had low confidence because of her abusive parents-in-law. After an initial period of home visits, she began attending a parenting group run by Lihn (herself Vietnamese) structured around parenting skills such as cooking, craft and toddler behaviour: 'We come to her house many times and she reduced her anxiety and she doesn't feel lonely. And after that we normally get the people to the group, and in the group first she was very shy, didn't have a friend, but after that she got a friend.' At the end of each session they would share a modest lunch of Vietnamese food. Lihn proudly recounted an instance where another woman – a victim of domestic violence living in a refuge – said at the end of her first shared meal, 'Wow, I feel like I'm back to my family in Vietnam'.

Aaron was similarly enthusiastic about the relationship between parents initiated in a fathers' group: 'So, four months in, there were fathers that were supporting other fathers even outside the programme. So they would go and see each other on the weekends and they would go play.' Ideally, users would 'exit' such programmes with stronger informal support networks that would supplant the need for formal service provision. This approach reflects the legacy of a broader emphasis on social capital and community-building in social policy (Leonard and Onyx, 2004).

'Helping people to help themselves' was also a recurring mantra across the range of services I encountered, from clinical services to soft-entry programmes. Staff consistently articulated their responsibility as being to *enable* client access, engagement and autonomy. The aim of developing the autonomy and confidence to manage challenges was apparent when staff somewhat reluctantly described the responsibilities welfare users ought to fulfil when accessing the service:

Alima: Um, and I think also, just the homework. So basically therapy isn't just about what we do here for half an hour, once a week or once a fortnight – it's largely with … you know, empowering the parents to be able to go home and practice the skills and incorporate them into daily activities. Some parents are fantastic and some parents [pause], um, they mean well and they try their best, but maybe they're just finding it, yeah, difficult to do, and they just want it fixed when they come.

Marika: Expectations, responsibilities? Um [pause]. I guess we empower families – if there does need to be a follow-up outside the session. So empowering families to have the responsibility to be able to follow that up.

Ali: I would just hope that they would be open and truthful with things and that they would commit to some of the sessions as well.

These quotes from early-career practitioners show the professional vocabulary of 'empowerment', in this case associated with an enabling approach that aims to equip service users with the skills and connections to act for their own benefit.

Matilda, a more experienced practitioner, elaborated on how she embedded enablement in her professional practice:

'[S]ay in the past a family might say to me, "Oh …" – I'm giving a real example here from a month ago – a family would say, "Oh, I don't know how my child goes at that childcare centre. They said he cries, I don't know how he's going, if he's getting better or if …" So there was a time when you might think, "Okay, I'll call the centre and find out for the family, and tell the family". And I think that we are really challenging that in our practice, and thinking, how do I support that parent to problem solve and find the best way to connect with the centre.'

Matilda went on to describe coaching the parents to arrange a time to speak to the director of the childcare centre themselves. Her example showed the effort it takes to translate the principle of empowerment into practice. She named this effort as part of her professional responsibility to strengthen service user capacities for problem-solving and self-advocacy.

Most staff identified showing up to a scheduled appointment or cancelling the appointment in advance as the primary responsibility of service users, avoiding a waste of limited resources:

Marika: You know, when you do develop rapport, they're unable to make an appointment or they need to, you know, change, or if circumstances come up, that they're able to, um, to notify us ... I guess, let us know when they can. Um, expectations? [pause], I guess yeah, and with them notifying us if they're unable to come, I guess, that kind of builds respect for the service as well.

Matilda: Um, in terms of the families that I am working with, I guess you could say, you know, their responsibility is perhaps, to show up to an appointment that we've made. But I still feel that, you know, if I have communicated really well with a family, and they can't make it or something happens, they will ring me. Um, so failure to attend doesn't happen all that much.

Marika and Matilda implied that they were answerable for their ability to build rapport and foster communication in a way that enabled service users to show up. Putting personal engagement and relationship-building at the heart of empowering service provision is consistent with contemporary critical social work (see Fook, 2012).

The more experienced workers I spoke to emphasised the interpersonal and communication skills required to carry off their professional responsibilities, such as reflexivity, listening to user perspectives, seeing users' life in context and avoiding expert hubris. Irene, who had spent her entire working life in the community sector, explained the importance of 'the person who drives the programmes' above and beyond the policy:

'[T]o be able to pick up the cues of when families are feeling not comfortable. And building strategies to ensure that, you know, that they can link with you and feel confident that. ... And being honest,

I think sometimes as professionals we're a little bit too … want to project we're the know-it-alls. I mean, just tell them, 'I don't know the answers, but I've got a good set of ears. I'll listen to you' . … Just don't patronise them. Yeah, they're down and out, and they know it before you know it. They know it more than you know it.'

Matilda similarly explained her role of enabling access at the coalface of service delivery:

'So I am currently funded by the government to offer this service and I want to make sure that there are no barriers, as few barriers as possible, for families to access this government-funded service. And so, I need to look at policies and procedures, but also the way I conduct myself, [for example] in a phone call, to make sure that I optimise families' opportunities to access this service. I've probably given quite few examples of this along the way. Um, and that's you know, my responsibility, and also to support families to access other opportunities in their community.'

Matilda saw her primary goal and responsibility as minimising barriers to service access and linking people into wider social networks, a dual obligation to government funders on the one hand, and local communities on the other. Her attitude reflected the increasing recognition that the way services are run and delivered may make them inaccessible, rather than focusing on the preferences and behaviours of people who don't take up services (Cortis et al, 2009).

While these workers described themselves as the bearers of this responsibility, its objective was to draw out the latent capacities and imminent self-responsibility of service users. The latter were expected to reciprocate by respecting the limited resources of the service and cancelling appointments if they couldn't make it, applying professional direction in their daily lives, and being open and truthful in their encounters with services.

The problem of access is vulnerable and isolated clients under-accessing or not accessing available supports; the goal of facilitating access is to draw people into networks of support and build their skills and confidence to manage. Having the confidence to ask for help and navigate the system is a sign of empowerment. But it can be a fine line between client assertiveness being read as empowered or over-entitled by frontline staff.

Knowing how to work the system (negative access)

Where access was mentioned as an excess rather than absence of engagement, the main but not exclusive reference point was Emergency Relief. Even workers from organisations that did not deliver Emergency Relief tended to use it as the example of inappropriate access and undue entitlement. Welfare users who were familiar with the available aid – when and where to access it – were often described as 'knowing the tricks' or 'knowing how to work the system'.

Emergency Relief programmes distribute material and financial crisis aid, typically food or transport vouchers, part-payment of outstanding rent or utility bills, or household goods and food parcels. Programmes also offer budgeting assistance, advocacy and referrals. At the time of my research, the Commonwealth government had provided Emergency Relief grants to 300 community and charity organisations across Australia (Department of Social Services, 2015). Generally, applicants attend an appointment and describe the challenges they are facing, presenting proof of their financial and family situation – usually in the form of a Centrelink (Department of Human Services) statement that states income, relationship status and number of dependants. The number and frequency of requests an applicant had made and the level of assistance received is tracked on a register.

Some workers were emphatic that familiarity with available assistance betrayed ungracious expectation and opportunism. Anthony was vocally and vehemently critical of what he saw as some service users' treatment of Emergency Relief as an income supplement. I queried this by asking him if it might indicate that the meagre income support people receive is insufficient to live on, particularly in an expensive city like Sydney. He was certain payments were sufficient and, what's more, some welfare recipients get more through their suite of benefits than community workers earn.

I heard this claim a number of times from different staff, invariably using the same example of a family with one partner receiving the Disability Support Pension, the other Carer Payment, and with many dependants. Besides fixating on only two payment types, the assumption that they are lucrative disregards the higher needs and costs associated with disability (Saunders, 2007). When taking into account actual income received and the cost of housing, many recipients of the Disability Support Pension still fall below the poverty line, even if they fare better by this measure than recipients of other major payments (Li et al, 2019).

Anthony described a time he saw a client smoking in the street, adding, 'They need financial help but apparently they can afford cigarettes'. His tone seemed to at once assume my agreement, but also that he was teaching me a thing or two about 'the reality out there'. Welfare recipients misspending taxpayer money is an axiom of welfare politics. While Anthony's was a hard-line opinion among the people I spoke to, other workers (and sometimes welfare users themselves) who were more sympathetic to the hardships of living on support payments expressed versions of the same sentiment.

Other workers felt that knowing what was on offer revealed something more ambiguous about entitlement and deservingness. Sandra was far more torn about questions of expectation and access than Anthony. Emergency Relief was also her reference point when it came to describing welfare-savvy people who know the 'tricks':

Sandra: I do feel the more … the earlier people receive support, the more support they'll get. They become more, obviously more aware of the services about, and the benefits on offer. I don't mean specific to Centrelink benefits but a whole range of benefits; and so there probably would be some individuals, and this would be the minority, that for, want of a better expression, do know how to work the system.

Emma: Do you have any examples you can give me?

Sandra: Well, I guess Emergency Relief.

Sandra's uncertainty lay in the fact that those already tapped into available support would make the most of it. A canny welfare user was the opposite of someone who was hard-to-reach.

But she still thought that an underlying need drove them to 'make it their business to work out' what was on offer and how they could benefit from it:

'Yeah, so, Emergency Relief, you know, there's the pot of money that organisations get to distribute Emergency Relief. But people will still, if they feel that they can get assistance will make a call into that organisation. But we will get calls, because we are a community organisation. So you refer them to where they can get that stuff, including Emergency Relief. But sometimes they know specifically the agencies. Well they are in need of assistance. I guess, even the people that know how to work the system, they're working the system because they do need help. You wouldn't have people who were comfortable, just doing it for fun. They do need help.'

She told me about receiving phone calls from 'cluey' individuals who know which agencies to go to, which agencies they've gone to already and how long they have to wait between visits: 'They're aware of that, it's not like a one-off thing, you know.'

Sandra suggested that 'knowing the tricks' demonstrated both familiarity with the system and sufficient need to bother working it. I asked another worker whether this was an example of resourcefulness and the kind of initiative they tried to instil in the people they served. She replied that it did demonstrate resourcefulness, but ultimately it was unproductive as people get stuck in the cycle of looking for short-term relief instead of looking for work to lift themselves out of their present circumstances. Whether interpreted as resourcefulness or opportunism, familiarity with the system was viewed as indicative of a cycle of dependency.

It wasn't accessing support per se that some staff considered problematic. Rather, it was accessing material aid without making use of additional support programmes, described as expecting 'a handout, rather than a hand up'. When I asked Rina what obligations service users accessing support should demonstrate, she said it depended on the person's situation. Again, Emergency Relief was the example she offered. If someone was accessing crisis assistance regularly, she would say 'Okay, I'm able to help you, but there's another programme you need to see, like a financial counsellor'. Signing up to other programmes isn't an official condition of receiving assistance, but because aid is given at the discretion of staff they can push for it (or not): 'It's not a condition, but as an encouragement to improve themselves and to put that idea in their mind how to improve themselves with our support.' Rina viewed this as a matter of good practice – getting at the root of the crisis – as well as fairness – using a limited budget to 'provide support for everyone'.

Fadi viewed disinterest in engaging with support programmes as a sign of 'taking the system for granted' and 'lack of initiative'. He contrasted lack of interest and initiative with people who show gratitude and fortitude:

> 'There are people that are actually wanting to engage with you, so when you come they're asking you all these questions and it's nice to know that there are people like that because sometimes you feel like a lot of people do take advantage of what we do here. Like, we've got Emergency Relief where people can come in for a food voucher and some people will come here [after the required interval] to the day, on the day they'll be here because that's when they're eligible.
>
> Then other people, you know, you see that it's been a year or so when you do give them a call and you say, "I just want to see how you're going" and that's where they're like, "I've been really struggling" and then you tell them, "Did you know you're eligible for another voucher?" and then they get excited and they're like, "Thank you so much. This is going to help me so much" and, yeah, so there are people more responsible that they make a genuine effort, they just happen to be in not the best of circumstances at the time.'

For Fadi and Rina, like other workers I spoke to, expectation signalled lack of appreciation. As Rina put it, 'some people don't appreciate because they have expectation of the welfare'.

The problem of access, then, was one of improper use and over-access, predominantly associated with material and financial aid. Repeatedly accessing aid was seen to demonstrate dependency and failure to 'get it together'. Frontline workers were prone to interpret users in this way when they did not reciprocate by demonstrating obvious gratitude, by enrolling in additional capacity-building programmes, or by accepting their professional direction.

My point is not to deny that there are people whose knowledge of and familiarity with the system allows them to squeeze what they can out of it. Rather, I'm interested in how taking action to access support is coded as either a positive or negative trait, and how this breathes new life into the long-held distinction between the 'deserving' and 'undeserving' poor.

Evaluating positive and negative access

Welfare users capable of navigating the system feature in the positive and negative version of access outlined earlier – as both the goal and the problem of access (see Table 4.1). On the one hand, access is a central goal of the reordering of services as receptive and responsive to those most in need but hardest to engage. Policy and programmes aim to draw disengaged and isolated clients into networks of support and equip them with the skills and confidence to self-advocate and self-manage. Staff framed their professional responsibility as facilitating access at the coalface of service delivery. On the other hand, welfare users knowing how to access resources and initiate that access is defined as a persistent problem of service provision. Whether seen as betraying undue entitlement and ingratitude or genuine need, it was read as a sign of a deeper passivity and dependency.

The 'problem of access' demonstrates how recipients of support are expected to act in order to be validated as in need and deserving. Ideal access was characterised by 'deserving vulnerability' and 'empowered responsibility'. 'Deserving vulnerability' points to the ways in which 'the vulnerable' become the legitimate targets and consumers of limited resources; 'empowered responsibility' points to the desired outcome of activating the welfare user's ownership over meeting their needs. These terms indicate the moral assumptions at play in ideas of vulnerability and responsibility – to be deserving is to be unassuming, grateful, to show evident suffering and fortitude. Ideal recipients humbly accept direction but also actively pursue improvement. This echoes Mark Peel's (2003) description of 'performing poverty', where the poor are expected to exhibit a balance of suffering, gratitude and unbeaten resolve (this is explored from the perspective of welfare users in Chapter 5). Linking the concepts of vulnerability and responsibility to the framing of access refines our understanding of the broader paradigms that shape how poverty must be performed.

Moral judgements are often explicitly called for in welfare delivery, but they can also be an unintentional side effect of the people-processing work

Table 4.1: The polarised problem of access

Positive access	Negative access
More access = goal	Too much access = problem
Initiative as responsibility	Initiative as opportunism
Receptive to professional direction	Rejects professional direction
Access to social networks	Access to material aid
Empowerment	Dependency

of frontline services (Lipsky, 2010). Categorisation is part and parcel of human service work; categories formally demarcate the characteristics that qualify or disqualify people from accessing provisions (Lipsky, 2010: 105). More generally, humans group things, people and practices to make sense of and evaluate their world. The compulsion to categorise – whether in everyday social life or through formal bureaucratic processes – comes before the stereotypes or social divisions that shape the classifications we come up with (Sayer, 2005: 143; Lipsky, 2010: 115).

Fleshing out judgement as an emotional and bodily practice might help account for the resonance of certain scripts of access – like 'deserving vulnerability' and 'empowered responsibility' – with frontline workers. Evaluation is not always a deliberate and considered assessment; it may be a spontaneous and unconscious feeling about something or someone (Sayer, 2005: 139). Sociologist of class, Andrew Sayer (2005), understands moral evaluations not as a formal set of standards but as embodied and emotional orientation ranging from subtle feelings of 'ease and unease' to strong feelings of 'approval or revulsion' (Sayer, 2005: 139). Anthropologist Tess Lea (2012: 110) sees bureaucracies as made up of people who 'think, feel, and emote', showing how boredom and pleasure can bring to life frontline work as much as rational deliberation.

Frontline staff judged welfare users as reciprocating when they displayed qualities valued by staff, including emotive qualities such as gratitude and receptivity. The examples I have drawn together suggest that particular demeanours and dispositions may be more readily read as reciprocating – like deference and gratitude – and therefore interpreted as conforming to ideal scripts of access. Other qualities – such as over-familiarity and 'refusing' to engage – may be taken as indicative of expectation and entitlement. The distinction Janet made between second-generation Arabic-speaking women and newly arrived migrants shows how visceral cues become entangled with cultural stereotypes that stick to some bodies more than others (Amin, 2010; Abdel-Fattah, 2016). She contrasted the supposed arrogance of 'loud and showy' second-generation Arabic-speaking women with the newly arrived migrants who were unfamiliar with the system and willing and grateful recipients of assistance.

Judgements about access don't simply hinge on the characteristics of welfare users; they also relate to how staff see or want to see themselves. Janet's characterisation of second-generation Arabic-speaking mothers suggested discomfort about professional expertise in a way that connected to wider scripts about difference and belonging. Puzzling over their low rate of participation in welfare services, she said:

> 'There's no language barrier because they speak English since they were born here. And sometimes I felt like, "well it's not me". Because I've been thinking, those women probably think "I speak more English than you do. How do you know much?" Because I speak English with accent, and I'm from another culture. But when they got to know me, they just started realising that I do know lots of things. But then, I've been thinking, my colleagues they were Anglo-Australian, and they've been here for years in the field, and the participation rate from this particular group is as low as mine, probably even lower; so it's nothing to do with me.'

Her response gave away a certain anxiety about their perception of her ability to give advice as a migrant whose relationship to the country was different from her Australian-born clients. She worried that her foreign accent implied lack of familiarity and professional knowledge, but was reassured that her Anglo-Australian colleagues encounter similarly low participation in the programmes they run. Her assertion that these mothers are arrogant because 'they speak English' had particular significance given her own anxieties about their perception of her as foreign, and therefore unknowledgeable. This example shows how staff imagine their professional identity through the construction of welfare users and their relationship to them.

Who initiates 'empowerment' can also influence how staff interpret initiative. Matilda described the professional discomfort that can arise when clients push for a preferred approach, suggesting it can be 'a fine line' between interpreting a client's initiative as presumptuous or empowered. She gave the example of a family asking for a support letter for social housing, and a colleague responding, 'You know, they're just using you. Don't do that letter for them'. When I asked her what determined the crossing of that line, she illustrated by mimicking the comments of colleagues: 'In fact, any act of empowered behaviour, unless I've given it to you and created it in you – in that case I like it – but if you have come up with it yourself, you're stepping over the line a little bit there.' The push–pull of professional and client agency as the locus of change – whereby practitioners are cast as responsible for eliciting personal responsibility in welfare users – seems to be one of the tipping points between positive and negative access.

Teach a man to fish

Michael Lipsky (2010) (originally published in 1980) influentially argued that policies take shape through the decisions and interpretation of workers on the front line of service delivery. He showed how work conditions characterised by ambiguous organisational goals and inadequate resources encourage 'street-level bureaucrats' to develop routines and strategies – including bias – to cope with the gap between the ideal of the work they carry out and what they can actually achieve. Lipsky's account has more recently been developed to acknowledge the professional values that motivate practitioners and shape their judgements, which can conflict with organisational goals (Ellis, 2011; Evans, 2011).

The conflicted conditions of contemporary welfare provision are embodied in the hackneyed saying, 'Give a man to fish and you feed him for a day; teach a man to fish and you feed him for a lifetime'. A few times workers referred to this saying to explain the principles underpinning community welfare. Rina responded to my question about service users' obligations: 'So they have that responsibility because we're here to help them, not to provide the fish for them [but] to teach them how to fish then they're able to go and fish for themselves.' Despite their various positions, the staff I interviewed shared a sense that their job was to instil and encourage service users' capacity to manage their own lives and have greater input into meeting their own needs. The saying captured a shift in the priorities of social policy from providing economic relief to cultivating people's skills and experiences.

This saying strikes a chord with divergent meanings of 'empowerment', which is widely used to describe the purpose and process of the helping professions. 'Teach a man to fish' could conjure the more expansive vision of wellbeing that welfare economist Amartya Sen (1999) famously calls 'flourishing'. Sen (1999: 87) acknowledges that low income is not the only factor that undermines capabilities, although he still sees economic resources as necessary for converting opportunities into outcomes. An alternative version of the story is that economic relief gets in the way of empowerment. 'Give a man a fish and you feed him for a day' chimes with the argument that welfare produces a 'culture of dependency', which has been used to justify conditioning, if not withdrawing, direct provision of support because it is incapacitating (Mead, 1997). The apparent wisdom of the saying obscures its context; control of production to achieve subsistence is a misleading analogy given the low-skill, low-pay jobs the poor are actually pushed to take up.

The problem of access speaks to the tension between providing relief and building capacities that has been a preoccupation of welfare reforms over the last four decades. The language of 'empowerment' is susceptible to co-option by anti-State and pro-market agendas that promote self-responsibility at the expense of social responsibility (Kenny and Clarke, 2010). But empowerment initiatives are not reducible to any single agenda (Newman, 2010). Nor is it simply a matter of 'bad' market notions of empowerment and 'good' community development ideas of the term. The meaning of empowerment relates not only to the balancing act between government and organisational goals that community welfare workers must negotiate; it also strikes at the core of what it means to be a helper in the helping professions.

Sally, who had worked in a number of different roles in the community welfare sector, explained the importance of striking a balance between providing a safety net and a springboard for people living in difficult circumstances:

> 'You need to give some structure or perimeters of that support to move on, because there's a comfortability in being supported. When you're already in a place and you're quite vulnerable and you realise how vulnerable you are, and you feel like the worlds coming down and you're demotivated and all the other things that come with being vulnerable and disadvantaged. ... You need to feel reassured that there is something. You take respite in the belief that you'll be looked after for the short term, but then you're being supported to pick up your momentum, to move on.'

People needed to feel supported enough to pick themselves up and prevail, but not so supported that they became complacent or immobile.

Regardless of the motives of community services, service users may be unaware of or uninterested in policy and professional aspirations to empower. There are people who simply want practical help without the direction associated with it. Bill, an older Aboriginal man, was exasperated by the suggestion of financial counselling when he sought Emergency Relief: 'I say to them, "we don't get the finance to work the budget out."' Like others I spoke to, he saw his problem as lack of money, not an inability to budget. This highlights the possible discrepancy between what welfare users understand as empowerment and the normative assumptions of agencies and professionals.

Conclusion

The ideals of 'deserving vulnerability' and 'empowered responsibility' are compelling precisely because they are morally charged and malleable, appealing to the 'moral imagination' (Marston and McDonald, 2012) of staff working from both social justice and restrictionist visions of welfare (Brown, 2011). Creating accessible service networks is a key goal of community service provision, where access is envisioned as a positive portal to empower vulnerable, particularly isolated, members of the community by facilitating connection and building skills and confidence. On the other hand, access also figures as a key problem when clients know how to work the system and seek out services and resources where they can. Initiative and confidence to navigate the system are part of both versions of the problem, yet in the former it is a product of empowerment and in the latter a sign of underlying dependency. Polarised understandings of welfare users' 'cynical manipulation' or 'vulnerability' also characterised Del Roy Fletcher and colleagues' (Fletcher et al, 2016) much larger study involving interviews with 45 national agency stakeholders and 27 focus groups with frontline welfare practitioners in England and Scotland. Many key stakeholders considered accounts of gaming the system to be exaggerated, and deployed narratives of vulnerability to challenge the disproportionate impact of sanctions on those whose agency they deemed compromised (Fletcher et al, 2016: 182).

Gratitude is the point where the problems of access and of cultural difference appear to intersect. Some cultural styles and demeanours become marked as arrogant and expectant and others as humble and receptive. This suggests that some bodies fit ideal scripts of access more readily than others. How staff in the community sector use, rework and challenge these ideals is indicative not simply of personal or professional assumptions about and attitudes to need and entitlement, but a broader cultural and economic politics of access that structures the distribution of material resources.

I don't want to overstate how ideals of fair and empowering access determine delivery of services and material aid. The criteria for determining access depend on the specific programme, organisation and funding arrangements. For example, the bureaucratic administration of social security payments is based on different principles of access than family support programmes delivered by non-profits. Yet practitioners' judgements can still influence user experiences of accessing support even if they have no bearing on technical eligibility, as I show in the following chapter.

5

Negotiating vulnerability

I was in the thick of my fieldwork when *Struggle Street* aired in 2015. The television documentary about poverty in the western Sydney suburb of Mount Druitt was controversial from the outset. Before its release, residents who participated in the show accused it of ridiculing them in a promotional video that showed them passing wind, swearing and shouting. A convoy of garbage trucks converged on SBS studios – a public broadcaster – to protest the 'garbage programme' and to tell the public 'we love Mount Druitt'. The Mayor of Blacktown City Council, which encompasses the suburb, accused the producers of encouraging participants to perform certain activities to manufacture the drama. After its release, public commentators debated whether the show was a classic example of 'poverty porn' or an unflinching portrait of 'life on the fringes'.

Described by the producers as a 'fly on the wall documentary', *Struggle Street* relied on the candour, generosity and performance of the residents who told their stories and agreed to be followed by the camera. The details of their hardship – the everyday disruptions and obstacles – rang painfully true to my own experience of growing up poor, and living with friends and family who remained so. I was struck by how readily they lay bare the details of their lives before the camera, how the details were offered as justification of why they lived like they did, and why their lives hadn't turned out differently.

Sixteen-year-old Bailee, for example, provides a matter-of-fact account of family violence, homelessness, depression and attempted suicide. She leads the film crew through her vandalised public housing flat, so trashed that the lease had been terminated, leaving her homeless again. Later, the camera stays with her as she explains to a local youth worker that she was raped after being kicked out of home at 13, and that she started using 'ice' (a form of methamphetamine). The male narrator (David Field), with his broad Australian accent, insists on a clichéd commentary that imposes on the mundane directness of her account – 'and that's how it is when you're on the fringe'.

Despite the ridiculing tone of the promo, the documentary itself offers a sympathetic insight into the banal drama that complicates life in poverty, albeit one that veers into voyeurism of the strange antics of the poor. It provides a window into the instability of poverty at the same time as it embodies the persistent pressure on those living in hardship to describe it in convincing detail.

I watched this dynamic play out on screen and in my fieldwork as I spoke to and spent time with people at the sharpest end of Australia's welfare system. These were people who had relied on social security for many years and were surrounded by friends and family who also relied on public payments to get by. They were the most marginal of the welfare users I spoke to, many of them routinely in contact not only with Centrelink, but also with various non-governmental organisations (NGOs) that deliver employment and family services or administer government-funded Emergency Relief. The expectation that they divulge the details of their hardship came from many directions, from welfare agencies demanding proof of neediness and worthiness to well-meaning researchers, like myself, intent on giving voice to their situations.

The relationship between experiencing and describing hardship is central to debates about the value of understanding hardship in terms of 'vulnerability'. Critical scholars have shown how 'vulnerability' operates in social policy to caste certain social groups – such as people with disabilities, queer youth and Aboriginal people – as at risk by virtue of their minority identity. They argue that the idea of 'vulnerability' works in tandem with 'risk' and 'resilience' to define social problems in terms of individual characteristics rather than social conditions. 'Vulnerable populations' become the target of interventions to change individual behaviour and keep difference in check. Despite these shortfalls, others insist that the concept of 'vulnerability' is still useful for understanding the relationship between individuals and the wider forces that shape their lives. All human beings are susceptible to suffering and harm, but this is made worse by the inequities of the societies they live in or made better by responsive social institutions (Misztal, 2011; Mackenzie et al, 2014; Fineman, 2016).

These understandings of vulnerability are not mutually exclusive. Both angles recognise that social policy may create vulnerability by promoting 'neglect and suffering' at the same time as it holds the 'promise of good care' necessary to reduce vulnerability (Gill et al, 2017: 4). Here I attempt to bridge these perspectives by holding in view both the classification of long-term welfare recipients as 'the vulnerable' and the lived condition of vulnerability that can characterise deprivation. I do so in an effort to treat this popular buzzword critically without losing sight of the genuine adversity it is intended to signal.

The most marginal welfare users I encountered negotiated vulnerability in their everyday life – although they rarely named it as such – in the form of practical hurdles and personal indignities. Cultural scripts and daily experiences of vulnerability intersected in the expectation that welfare recipients routinely rehearse the everyday challenges they faced in a way that is recognisable as genuine and deserving. For some, the performative demands of welfare agencies created yet another hurdle that could potentially trip them up or leave them exposed, adding insult to the injury of deprivation.

'We struggle everyday'

Kat was an Aboriginal woman in her 50s living on Disability Support Pension (DSP). She lived with her young adult sons in public housing. When her oldest son was released from prison without medication or a prescription, it created 'a big drama' for the family. Kat managed to get her son a last-minute appointment with her doctor to obtain a script, but the medication wasn't typically stocked in pharmacies and had to be ordered in. 'It was a big runaround trying to find his mediation', she explained. Circling back to an earlier question I'd asked about what makes a supportive family, Kat described how her daughters were embroiled in the drama: 'Again, with the family support, the girls were on the phone trying to get it from different chemists, which we did. We ended up finding it over [name of a suburb] way.' Tracking down the medication absorbed their attention and energy. A relatively minor complication created significant stress, particularly because it held the threat of a more explosive medical episode.

For Kat and some of the other people I interviewed, daily life was chequered by the unrelenting pressure of 'just surviving' and 'big drama' that could threaten to undo them. People told me of intense and tragic challenges associated with illness, substance abuse or domestic violence. People talked – sometimes casually – of fleeing a violent partner with their children, hospitalisation for drug addiction or mental illness, a psychotic episode, incarceration, drug overdose or a heavy loss on the poker machines. It's worth remembering that the number and range of people I sought out were not intended as representative, so I'm not claiming that these issues are typical of life on welfare. But the long-term recipients I spoke to were most often touched by one or more of these problems, whether they were going through them personally or knew someone who was.

They also confronted a different scale of disruption, which was less sensational. The kinds of mundane disruptions I heard about included an over-drawn bank account that incurs a penalty and throws out the fortnightly budget, not having money for the train fare to a compulsory job network appointment, the breakdown of household appliances that there's no money to replace, a Centrelink review of benefits entitlement or sanction for not complying with mutual obligation requirements, shortage of money because it was spent on school photos or an excursion, the cost of medication not covered by the Pharmaceutical Benefits Scheme (PBS) or referral to an expensive specialist,[1] paying a fine, getting caught shoplifting, losing your driver's license or an infected tooth. These incidents created disproportionate disarray and sapped disproportionate energy.

Kathleen Millar (2014: 34) uses the concept of 'everyday emergencies' to refer to the multiple insecurities that destabilise daily life in the Brazilian favelas she studies. The concept points to the way that insecurity does not simply interrupt, but rather, is part of normal life in Rio's slum neighbourhoods. Everyday emergencies are unexceptional to the people experiencing them, but they look from the outside like an exceptional breakdown of the normal order of things. While Millar uses 'everyday emergencies' to capture the immediacy of daily disruptions, it strikes a chord with the impending and 'unrealised' quality of vulnerability (Brown, 2011: 319). Sociologists have included the fear and uncertainty of being tipped into future crisis without the possibility of help as a central aspect of vulnerability (Emmel and Hughes, 2010: 177). The inherent unpredictability of individual life is compounded by insecure income and social support (Misztal, 2011). The concept of 'everyday emergencies' usefully points to the ordinariness of insecurity and the heightened exposure to crisis it creates.

For the most marginal welfare users I spoke to, daily life in poverty consisted of a series of everyday emergencies that were mundane but had the potential to blow up and wreak havoc. They included the routine potholes and hurdles of getting by on a meagre income and the more tumultuous episodes of violence or illness. As Kat's example shows, the mundane slog of getting by and the urgency of crisis could be closely entangled. Despite their ordinariness, everyday emergencies could still wear people down or leave them reeling.

While most people I spoke to had to be careful with money, for others it was a daily struggle to find food or pay bills. As Reem, a Lebanese-Australian single parent of three, said, holding back tears: 'We struggle every day. ... But what do you do? You've just got to keep going.' Bill, an older Aboriginal man on the Age Pension, described the daily struggle to provide for his family:

'But it gets you down because honestly there's not a day that goes by that I'm [not] under pressure for food. Not a day that goes past. ... Oh a lot of times I've got to come to [family support worker] and she'll get us food and things like that. It's just – everything is in bills. I'll get caught because I can't pay the whole bill. I can pay some of it and then I might leave say $50 short or $70 short. So the next time it comes, well that $50 adds on and then I find out I can't [afford it] so I've got to say "oh well, I'll have to pay the other $100 next time".'

Just as expected daily costs could accumulate and get out of control, unexpected costs could also be very disruptive and destabilising. Monica was an Anglo mother in her late 20s who had relied on Parenting Payment (PP) (single) since she had her daughter in her late teens. She told me how a deduction from her payment had left her unable to budget for Christmas. She was entitled to child support from her daughter's father and, even though she hadn't received any, Centrelink still determined that they had overpaid her and begun deducting from her fortnightly benefit in the lead-up to Christmas. Greg was an Anglo man who had just become eligible for the Age Pension but was previously a long-term recipient of the Newstart Allowance (unemployment benefit). He lost the boost in income to a repayment plan for an overblown water bill caused by a hidden leaking pipe, which the council insisted he pay at the maximum rate he could 'spare'.

People told me about not being able to plan ahead, but constantly having to think ahead to contain potential problems. Monica's account of 'rationing' food illustrates how this sense of planning permeates the most mundane tasks:

'[E]verything I do or use, I'm always thinking about the expense. ... You know, I always get cranky at my brother for instance, if I've just bought a new hot chocolate container he will go and have three scoops because it's a new jar. But that means three cuppas to me, like so I'm always thinking ahead. You have to think [ahead], like you have to, like to be able to budget you have to actually contemplate how you're going to make whatever last this many days.'

Bill similarly described the uncertainty of not knowing how he would feed himself or his children day to day: 'Every day I get up I've got to worry. Worry about where the loaf of bread's coming from. Worry about where the bottle of milk's coming from. Every single day. You just can't survive even these days.' Monica and Bill were absorbed by the demands of the present while the uncertainty of the future pressed in.

It's not hard to imagine how containing everyday emergencies might compete with the commitment to find work for those who were seeking it. As Millar (2014: 35) puts it, precarity is not always a matter of insecure work disrupting life: 'unstable daily living destabilizes work'. For example, Monica felt torn in different directions by her ambition to do something more with her life for her and her daughter's sake, the chaos of her siblings' problems, and the turmoil of her own bad relationships and drug addiction (her story is shared at length in the following chapter). She reflected on her conflicted commitment to her troubled family, 'I can't separate myself not to be part of their misery, I suppose'. The immediate priorities of getting by and the obligations to family and friends embroiled in everyday emergencies could trump or derail the desire and effort to get ahead.

Of course, the claim that unstable daily life gets in the way of work depends on how work is understood and valued. Making meagre resources stretch and jumping through the hoops of an increasingly conditional welfare system certainly involves time and energy. Stereotypes about idle and irresponsible welfare dependents also make invisible the work of caring for friends, family and community. What's more, priorities may be shaped by culturally oriented 'values, social obligations, and desires' other than mainstream employment (Gibson, 2010: 135).

Unlike Monica, Kat expressed little discomfort about receiving welfare benefits and being unemployed. Success to her meant being there to fulfil the needs of friends and family, but also being open to approaching others for help rather than suffering alone. 'Speaking for myself, I would just be helpful and being there for people; never being afraid to ask for things', she told me. But concluding that Aboriginal people like Kat don't regard regular work as a social responsibility would misunderstand the different meanings of work and obligation that shape their commitments (Gibson, 2010: 137).

Lorraine Gibson (2010) makes this point in her study of Aboriginal people's attitudes to paid employment in the remote New South Wales town of Wilcannia. Some of the regular disruptions to work that Gibson describes resemble the everyday emergencies I have drawn attention to here: 'Family illness, a hangover from a "big night on the drink", Nanna's need to do the shopping, the arrival of family and friends from out of town or an unexpected occurrence of interest continue to be the cause of much non-attendance at work' (Gibson, 2010: 135). She argues that these disruptions 'highlight the importance of family, not the unimportance of work'. Relationships to people, things and places – and the work that goes into sustaining them – defines identity in many Aboriginal cultures rather than occupation. Gibson reminds us that understanding how everyday emergencies affect work involves tuning in 'to the importance and nature of what "work" is' (Gibson, 2010: 137).

By naming the disruptions that occupy daily life in poverty 'everyday emergencies', my point is not to add to the air of crisis that breathes life into policy interventions in the lives of disadvantaged individuals and populations. The logic of intervention assumes that policymaking is orderly and disadvantaged lives are dysfunctional (Lea, 2012). Tess Lea unsettles this logic by showing the unruly side of policy work in Aboriginal health. In fact, she argues, concrete but ad hoc policy measures contribute to the disorder and disruptions of Aboriginal people's everyday life. This is an important insight given that the everyday emergencies people described to me so often related to the bureaucratic hoops and quagmires of claiming social security, not to mention the privations of living on such meagre payments. Lea insists that the urgency that grips the language of emergency and the rollout of intervention overlooks the banal and persistent 'duress' that has shaped everyday life for Indigenous people since colonisation began. The people who experience it are 'inured to dealing with the cruddy pragmatics of life' (Lea, 2012: 117).

The insecurity of daily life in poverty is a familiar story, but one that bears repeating. Without resources or options when things go wrong, even relatively minor challenges can quickly build up or spiral out of control. The focus becomes hanging on and surviving rather than aspiring and thriving. Robert Walker and his colleagues (2013: 223) describe this as being 'caught in the continuing short-term', while Mark Peel (2003: 69) articulates it as 'loss of movement towards the future'. But the future doesn't recede completely; its uncertainty looms large and without recourse. Everyday emergencies involve the immediate occupation of just surviving and the imminent threat of big drama. In this way insecurity unsettles yet settles into daily life in poverty.

'You gotta expose everything'

Kane and Nessa were two young Aboriginal friends, both in their mid-20s. Kane had dropped off the welfare rolls and wasn't working. He lived with his mother, who also lived on welfare payments. Nessa was a single mother receiving PP (single). When we sat down to interview, their familiarity and playfulness with each other compensated for their guardedness with me. I asked if they had ever found it hard to look after themselves or their family. 'Yeah' was Nessa's short and decisive reply. I gently prodded her for an example. 'Just daily basics. The struggle.' I awkwardly probed again. 'Could you describe it a little bit for me?' Her response was curt: 'I don't know, like bills, food, responsibilities. I have to care for children, so you gotta think of your children.' As a novice researcher, I was keen to draw out the texture and detail of everyday life. To Nessa, my questions and the details they aimed to elicit were frustratingly obvious and commonplace.

I was not the first person to ask Kane and Nessa to recite the details of their hardship. Those at the sharpest end of Australia's residual welfare system are required to routinely make a case for their poverty and to prove that they are both in need and deserving of support. As Mark Peel (2003: 72–3) explains:

'People in hardship must describe their lives all the time, often to someone who has the power to give or deny them something they need. This emphasis on proving need creates its own kind of convincing stories. ... You must be weak enough to have suffered yet strong enough to prevail.'

'Performing poverty' demands the appropriate display of suffering, unbeaten resolve and gratitude (Peel, 2003: 74). Kate Brown discusses 'performing vulnerability' in the context of delivering services to vulnerable young people. The professionals she interviewed associated vulnerability with disclosure of personal histories, 'contrition' for mistakes, 'compliance' and 'motivation for change' (Brown, 2014: 380). Youth who conformed to these expected behaviours were more likely to be classified as 'vulnerable' and benefit from support that status conferred. People participate in a particular 'telling' of their experience and circumstances in order to be recognised as needing social assistance.

Kane and Nessa resented having to give away personal information and peddle their own misfortune to increase their chances of getting support or avoid sanctions for non-compliance of mutual obligations:

Kane: Often if you go to them sorts of people [welfare agencies] you've gotta put it all out there, that you're homeless, that you got nothing, you got no friends, no family – and then they're gonna go boom 'alright' [you get the help you came for] …

Nessa: Yeah, that's what I had to do to get a house and it's embarrassing [talking over each other] I think it's embarrassing.

Kane: You gotta go down to those levels you know – it's wrong.

Nessa: When you gotta expose everything and don't want to, it's like your dignity.

Kane: Yeah, it's everything.

Kane and Nessa smarted at the retelling of these encounters more so than the other hardships they mentioned. Their palpable bitterness reflected a general change in demeanour during the interview as I steered the conversation toward the topic of government support. Kane slouched further in his chair, frowning and fidgeting with the information sheet I had given him. Nessa went from turning her phone over in her hand to holding it in front of her face, visibly texting as she responded to my questions. Their animated and playful responses to my questions about family gave way to a defensive yet defiant tone.

The burden on people seeking support to repeatedly talk about their struggles was not lost on some of the community welfare practitioners I spoke to. As Sally put it: 'They're coming again feeling ashamed. They've knocked on someone's door, to tell yet again how shitty their situation is.' Her response was to 'Talk to them, have a coffee, relax them. Once they get the anxiety out of the way, then introduce the paper and say "can you tell me your story?" Then [follow up with] "you've given me some insight, lets formalise your story a little bit"'. Sally's approach to listening to service users' stories would likely be affirming for some. Compare Kane and Nessa's experience to that of Kathleen, quoted by John Murphy and his colleagues (2011: 38), who tells a positive story about the worker conducting her Job Capacity Assessment:

'She validated my story … she said "tell me about the things that impact on your life, like I want to know your whole picture. And I need to have that evidenced by your doctor's report and your psychologist's report, so I need to know that you're not stooging me", which is okay, I'm happy to do that. But she said "I want to know the whole picture. And based on that, let's together work out a plan because I can hear that at some stage you want to, you want self-reliance and self-responsibility, but you need these things in order to do it".'

Kathleen was expected to 'tell everything' in a way that displayed both her misfortune and motivation. For Kathleen, who was new to the welfare system and who had applied for assistance for the first time after a divorce, this expectation was validating.

For Kane and Nessa, who were used to 'doing it tough' and had to describe their lives all the time, 'exposing everything' was another toll of poverty. They understood that reluctance to disclose could be interpreted as 'troublesome' even if the approach to service provision was supportive rather than suspicious (Clarke, Cheshire and Parsell, 2020: 265). While Kane and Nessa were perhaps the most eloquent at expressing the indignity of facing welfare agencies, a number of people in the worst hardship told me about having to explain 'the ins and outs' and feeling 'embarrassed', 'intimidated' or 'uncomfortable'. In a system where payments are conditional on fulfilling 'mutual obligation' requirements, recipients must regularly present to Centrelink or employment assistance agencies. For people in dire hardship, the frequency of the performance will likely be multiplied as extra relief is sought. The most marginal welfare recipients get a great deal of practice performing their hardship. Experience had taught Kane and Nessa the kind of role they were expected to perform and how to perform it.

Describing hardship before welfare agencies requires a particular performance of 'full disclosure', then, which taps into cultural ideas about what neediness – currently couched as vulnerability – is and looks like. Vulnerability morphs from a descriptor of social processes to a category of person – 'the vulnerable'. Categorisation allows welfare agencies – like other human services – to process people and determine who gets what and how they get it. Amorphous attributes – such as the right blend of misfortune and fortitude, deference and resolve – become markers of deserving vulnerability. Even more concrete is the use of risk assessment tools to assign individuals a category that determines the degree and form of professional intervention they receive (Caswell et al, 2010: 391). The classification of vulnerable individuals and populations can work against young Black men in particular as they are framed as not simply *at risk* but a *risk to* the community (Brown, 2014). Cultural ideas about vulnerability spell out criteria that make some welfare users more readily recognisable as needy and deserving than others.

But this does not guarantee that people will play their prescribed part. This was clear when I was invited by a community welfare provider to sit in on its Emergency Relief appointments. I sat perched in the corner of a small and barely furnished room on the staff side of a desk. Applicants would present their Centrelink income statement to a rostered staff member, who consulted and updated an agency database of previous applicants and decisions on a desktop computer. Even the small number of sessions that I observed was enough to demonstrate the different degrees to which people were willing to plead their exceptional circumstances. A few applicants were forthcoming, giving elaborate and animated descriptions of irregular circumstances and everyday emergencies. For example, one amenable applicant presented a large gas bill as evidence as she chattily explained that her sister had been evicted and there were two families living under the one roof, causing a surge in the household gas use. The applicant accepted a flyer about financial counselling and nodded in apparent assent as the Emergency Relief worker suggested turning down the temperature on the water heater to curb the use of gas.

Others, however, offered only the minimum information required of them. One applicant, when pressed by the Emergency Relief worker for details to justify extra assistance, insisted with quiet stubbornness that 'Centrelink isn't enough to live off and rent is too high'. This person withheld any other details and refused the offer of financial counselling. The applicant was technically eligible and was perhaps confident of this. Despite the worker's opinion that 'this person doesn't want to take responsibility' voiced afterward, the applicant left with the assistance sought. This example suggests that performing vulnerability does not amount to a straightforward exchange of convincing stories for a favourable outcome. In this case the Emergency Relief worker's power to give or deny assistance was limited by the concrete eligibility criteria, and yet the performative demands of the role of 'client' still cast a shadow over their interaction.

The fact that people living in poverty knowingly perform hardship suggests that stories of vulnerability may be actively used as resources in resource-constrained settings (Jansen, 2008). Kane indicated such insight by saying, 'you've got to put it all out there … and then they're gonna go boom "alright" (you get the help you came for)'. Frontline workers are likewise aware of the performative aspects of claiming support, as one Emergency Relief worker indicated by commenting, 'that woman dramatised her situation'. While this worker added 'that doesn't mean she wasn't genuine' as a qualification, the comment betrayed a degree of suspicion about exaggerated or fraudulent stories of hardship. Welfare users may deploy or disguise their vulnerability when accessing welfare services depending on the reception they anticipate (Midgley, 2018). An over-polished or over-performed story may attract suspicion rather than sympathy. However, 'performing vulnerability' does not equate with 'pretending'. The point is that experiences of hardship are more readily recognised and authorised as genuine and deserving when they are told in a particular cultural register.

While we might think of convincing stories of hardship as a resource in an economy of conditional welfare, we mustn't overstate the returns it garners or overlook the price it may incur. Increasingly targeted and conditional provision heightens the demand for proof and disclosure. Many benefit recipients must attend compulsory appointments, job search training courses, and – for the most marginal claimants – self-development and treatment programmes simply to receive their payments. In a welfare-to-work system that prioritises 'participation', frontline professionals have less leeway to respond to the needs of services users even though their role in assessing participation 'breaches' increasingly brings the most marginal and disadvantaged people before them (McDonald and Marston, 2006: 177). The rise of conditional welfare goes hand in hand with the heightened stigmatisation of poverty and welfare dependence (Tyler and Slater, 2018). Claiming social assistance under these conditions entails routine and systematic exposure without the promise of security in return.

The emphasis on proving need creates mutual mistrust. Sociologist Barbara Misztal foregrounds trust in her search for strategies to confront vulnerability. She argues that trust both produces and reduces vulnerability (Misztal, 2011: 120, 121). Trusting someone involves vulnerability because it requires faith that their intentions and actions will be in your interest without knowing the outcome. At the same time, strong relationships of trust can reduce vulnerability by creating confidence, security and hope. Misztal (2011: 122) points out that imbalanced relationships of dependency can breed mistrust and deception. Challenging the vulnerability arising from dependency therefore 'involves some real trust in the other party's goodwill and the proper use of discretionary power'. A welfare system that makes the promise of social security conditional rather than guaranteed institutionalises mistrust and further skews the asymmetrical relationship between providers and claimants of assistance.

The person seeking assistance is exposed in two ways: first, in laying bare the details of their hardship, and second, in relying on someone else's response. Kane articulated this twofold exposure, soon after adding: "Cos you got nothing else in that situation, you've put your heart on the line, told 'em everthink [sic], and now you're just sitting there waitin [sic] for something to happen. So it's up to them, they can go like that [clicks fingers] if they want to, and get you [trails off].'

Kane and Nessa felt let down by support services, especially employment agencies. As Nessa put it, 'the employment agency, they say "we promise you this, we promise you that" and they give you nothing'. And later in the interview, 'I don't trust em', 'cos they muck ya around'. Kane described the stress and lack of return that participation requirements like job search quotas, preparatory courses and mandatory appointments created: 'And it's like if I put this much time and effort into work I'd be getting way more [money], you know, and I'd be getting more out of it as well, instead of sitting in the office [of the employment agency] stressin [sic] out about the whole situation of getting paid.'

Kane and Nessa's mistrust also arose from the legacy of colonial abuse in the name of welfare. Welfare agencies have long been used to control Aboriginal people. Kane explained that the basics card 'comes back to the government controlling them [income-managed welfare recipients] because they've got control of that card'. Nessa was acutely aware of stereotypes about Aboriginal people as 'lazy dole bludgers': 'People think that Aboriginal people get free cars, free houses ... like ya lazy.' They bitterly resented how present-day income management policies characterised Aboriginal people as untrustworthy. It was little wonder Kane and Nessa were cynical about the goodwill of welfare agencies and their proper use of discretionary power.

Kane and Nessa's anger and resentment was contrary to the display of contrition, motivation and humble suffering that more readily indicates vulnerability within the dominant set of ideas about it. Based on our conversation, I doubt they would embrace vulnerability as a descriptor that applies to them (with the benefit of hindsight and experience, I wish I'd asked them directly). Rather than perform his expected role, Kane avoided the scene altogether. He had stopped receiving the unemployment benefit because he refused to participate in the 'muck around' requirements on which receipt of payment was conditioned. When I followed up Kane and Nessa's response with a question – 'How did you find the people who were helping you responded?' – Nessa boasted, 'Well I had a trainee, so yeah [proud] I told her what to do. [Wry laughter.] I got a house from telling her what to do'. She claimed her savviness as an asset in contrast to the ignorance of the trainee worker, signalling her own capacity to make things happen and inverting the negative view of 'working the system'. Nessa seemed to be reasserting her dignity after the exposure of admitting her indignity in front of me.

Acknowledging hardship

Not only do those at the sharp end of the welfare system have to endure the hardships of poverty, they also have to recite it in a way that is recognisable to others. When I asked Maureen, an Anglo woman in her 50s living on DSP, what she thought of the idea of everyday emergencies, she said: 'You don't have the flexibility that a rich person has to respond to crisis so you have to beg for help. That takes time! And you know you'll be judged like it's your fault.' Rebecca Stringer (2014) explains victim-blaming as a failed acknowledgment of wounding that further victimises sufferers, creating what she calls 'a second order vulnerability'. This is 'the ability to be wounded and then to have that wounding effaced, in language, by others, by law' (Stringer, 2014: 58). Facing welfare agencies and proving need can create the banal drama of everyday emergencies at the same time as exposing people to the secondary assault on their dignity.

But I don't want to reduce stories of hardship to their utility in an exchange with service providers. For one thing, performing vulnerability doesn't necessarily involve a transaction of concrete resources; sometimes it's about saving face and avoiding judgement. The performance can also be playful instead of painful. I remember sitting in the office of my high school guidance counsellor with my best friend. We were two of a handful of poor high-achievers in competition for a student bursary to help with the transition to university. We had sincerely told our stories about how we were determined to make it despite the struggles we faced. Neither of us had won the bursary and our guidance counsellor was checking in. As we prepared to leave his office, he casually offered us a scratchie with the $10 prize already unveiled, explaining that he had been gifted it by a parent. 'Sweet, we'll be eating tonight', I joked, looking to my friend as we both laughed. The concerned expression our guidance counsellor returned made the joke all the more enjoyable. We relished his earnest discomfort as we relived the moment on our walk home. Perhaps we were gently pushing back against his misplaced gesture, but I think we just enjoyed hamming up the role we'd been assigned. Of course, our ability to meet our needs was not on the line in that moment. We did not, in fact, depend on that scratchie to eat that night.

People also create a sense of who they are and the world around them through the stories they tell, both to themselves and others (Dunn, 2017). They do so by drawing on or pushing against wider narratives about what need and deservingness looks like. Monica, who received a charity Christmas hamper every year, talked about wanting to be 'on the other side of charity'. She did not extend compassion for those in need to herself: 'I really would like to be able to give to charity and give my time to them and my money to people who need it, not to be a charity case.' Monica was particularly thoughtful and articulate about her own self-narrative. I asked her what she would change about her life if she could, and she responded at length about removing her 'excuse making':

> I want to completely take the 'poor me' aspect out of my life because by saying 'poor me' I'm trying to take the focus off what I've done to put myself in this situation, and really, poor me? What's that do? Like that is not going to benefit me in any single way. If anything it's going to make me miserable by saying 'woe is me, look what happened'. Woopty-do, that's done, so learn from it and now – yeah, I just need to do what I know I can I suppose, and I'm not. I've been in the habit of just saying poor me and then trying to get understanding off other people and talking about it with other people who I know will agree.

For Monica, dwelling on her misfortune felt disempowering and offered little room or direction for change. Her faith in self-mastery gave her hope for an alternative future that energised and motivated her, but it also meant she keenly felt the sting of her problems as self-imposed.

While for Monica 'getting understanding off people' seemed like a way to avoid taking action, for Kat it was the opposite. She implied that she was less vulnerable now that she had learned how to find and ask for help: 'I think it's okay to ask other people for help and then that's how you learn to help yourself, yeah. Otherwise people don't know – you're just sitting there suffering or whatever when help is out there for whatever you may need.' She told me about a negative appointment with the State public housing authority. Under-investment in social housing in Australia makes public housing tenants among the poorest in the population, with huge waiting lists and unmet demand for others in need (Jacobs et al, 2010). Kat said an agency employee 'treated me like shit' when she enquired about housing repairs: 'She said, "Oh well you're lucky you got a house. You didn't wait for long." And again I've been there for 10 years and there's still no work.' Later in our interview she reflected: 'Well, back then I was vulnerable. If they had said that to me today I would have given them a piece of my mind and went higher. But I think Aboriginal people feel more intimidated and don't know where to go or what to do.'

This was the only time that someone I spoke to used the term 'vulnerable' to describe themselves. I had met Kat through a community welfare organisation so she had likely been in contact with the professional jargon. But her story also showed the strength she had gained from her willingness to ask for help and valuing it as a personal asset rather than a weakness. Kat experienced her growing capacity to stand up to welfare agencies as empowering, but some frontline staff might read her newfound assertiveness as overly familiar and expectant, as the previous chapter shows.

Conclusion

A key challenge of studying poverty and hardship is to sustain attention to the processes that entrench and exacerbate inequality without positioning suffering as the all-defining characteristic of those who bear the brunt of it. This challenge is at the heart of debates about the language of 'vulnerability' in social policy. The terminology we use to describe social conditions shapes the way we make sense of them. While some researchers, practitioners and advocates see the moral potency and explanatory power of 'vulnerability' as a force worth harnessing to promote social justice, others see it as politically fraught and likely to do more harm than good (Brown, 2011). Vulnerability tends to be a condition diagnosed by professionals but rarely by local communities themselves (Furedi, 2008: 242). I'm repeating the pattern by explaining the hardships of poverty in these terms, although I hope not uncritically.

A key problem associated with the language of vulnerability is the way it sticks to certain populations and defines them as necessarily at risk, disadvantaged or damaged. I have tried to incorporate this into an account of what long-term welfare users are vulnerable to, emphasising the relational dynamic of vulnerability as both a condition and a classification. Everyday emergencies disrupt yet dwell in everyday life, characterised by the mundane grind of poverty punctuated by crisis. In a system of welfare based on proof and disclosure, people are expected to recite these experiences as convincing and recognisable accounts of disadvantage. By destabilising daily life and demanding particular performances of hardship, Australia's increasingly meagre and conditional social security system contributes to the vulnerability of the most marginal welfare users even as it targets support at them.

6

The shame of protection

Reem was a second-generation Lebanese-Australian single parent living solely on Parenting Payment (PP) (single). 'I hate it, to tell you the truth', she told me. 'I hate asking for money, I hate asking for help. I would love to be able to do it on my own and to earn my own money. I just don't feel comfortable with it. Yes, I do receive money from Centrelink, but I don't feel comfortable.'

Like Reem, the people I spoke to often qualified their answer by expressing their discomfort when I asked how they felt about receiving welfare payments. Rhetoric about welfare recipients as 'dole bludgers' and 'tax burdens' insists there is little comfort to be taken in social security. Being comfortable with receiving welfare payments would betray an unforgivable sense of entitlement or lack of aspiration. Reem offered her feelings of unease as testament that she did not take income support for granted and was not resting on her laurels.

Like many studies of class inequality before it, shame ran through a number of my interviews. It was sometimes named outright, but more often expressed as failure, inadequacy, defensiveness, exposure or a sense of being misunderstood. The single mothers I spoke to were among the most keenly aware of being judged. Jasmin acknowledged that PP (single) helped supplement her part-time work and provide for her young children, but she avoided judgement by not telling people about it. She knew first hand how judgement worked: 'Before I had kids when I had a full-time job that's how I looked at single mothers too. I thought single mothers were just sitting in a coffee shop drinking and popping out kids. That's what I thought so I know they're judging me.'

Jasmin implied that part-time work shielded her from the judgement – 'That's why I work' – but she still 'felt useless' going from full-time employment to working part time and having children: 'It's different. From full time to part time, from making all this money, now I'm making $700 a fortnight and getting welfare.' Devaluing the work she *was* doing didn't seem to eat away at Jasmin, but it niggled at her sense of satisfaction and achievement. Assuming that life on welfare is idle and equating worth with paid work disregards other forms of commitment and effort, including care work and the work involved in claiming conditional welfare.

While shame surfaced to varying degrees in my conversations with a number of people, it consumed my separate interviews with Monica and Hasan. They were two individuals in very different circumstance, but both afflicted with a deep sense of shame about finding themselves in a position where they had to rely on the help of the Australian government – Hasan for asylum and Monica for a basic income. My initial interview with both of them was unusually long – close to three hours – and they were two of a handful of interview participants I stayed in touch with beyond the recorded interview. Shame seemed to drive their stories as a feeling that both overwhelmed and activated them. It was entangled with pride and their efforts to recover dignity. Here I retell Monica and Hasan's stories side by side and at length to maintain 'the context, history, and moral force' their narratives communicate (Osella and Osella, 2006: 571).

In Hasan and Monica's stories I see the tension between shame as both enabling and disabling that runs through academic literature on welfare, poverty and social class. There are two dominant and sometimes intersecting storylines in this literature – the common and crippling effects of shame on the one hand, and the different ways of dealing with welfare shaming on the other. Welfare politics and policies that blame the poor for their own misfortune are recognised as damaging wellbeing, but individuals are affected by the stigma of welfare to differing degrees and respond in a range of ways.

Like the topic of vulnerability more broadly, talking about the shame of welfare poses challenges for welfare researchers who want to call out the damaging effects of welfare systems without lumping all welfare recipients together as victims of those systems. This plays out in the ambiguous relationship between shame and agency, understood as the capacity to shape one's own life. The ability to develop and pursue one's own aspirations may be inhibited by chronic shame even as the cultural stereotypes, political scapegoating and bureaucratic humiliations of social security are actively negotiated. Through Hasan and Monica's stories, this chapter pays attention to the productive and destructive dimensions of shame, and disentangles the different capacities it makes possible or undermines. By zooming in on the details, a more complicated story of the shame of protection emerges.

Hasan's story

'I never dreamed of this, that I'll – one day I'll be coming to another country and begging them for the protection and asylum. This is what – it's a lot of guilt I have inside.'

When I first spoke to Hasan, his initial application for asylum in Australia had been denied and was before the Refugee Review Tribunal. Hasan and his family had to leave Pakistan because he had been terrorised and persecuted for being active in the Shi'a community of Sunni-majority Pakistan. At the time of our first meeting he had been in Australia for a year, living with a relative and working as a cleaner, having used up the family's savings. Despite the expense, his family had just moved into their own flat and he had recently found a job in a firm that made use of his skills as a consultant. Expensive rent, the high cost of living and the private lawyer fees for the review consumed most of the family's resources.

In Pakistan they had been wealthy. Hasan's job had come with perks like a car and health cover, his children attended private schools and his wife stayed home. Here, in Australia, they all worked – his wife as a cleaner and his teenage son in a chain store when he wasn't at school. Hasan was pragmatic about the need for his wife and son to work: 'In this country everybody has to work. That's fine. I'm now understanding the culture and everything. So mentally I'm prepared that everybody has to work in my family, except for my young one, because of survival.' He could reconcile it as a difference of culture and not just circumstance. The migration process lent itself to the interpretation of 'cultural difference' where difference was observed in a way that gave Hasan some relief from his anguish about not providing for his family.

Hasan was proud of his family pulling together to survive this tough time. And he was so proud of his children, who were flourishing:

Hasan: My son, obviously he's seen me working. He's seen his lavish life in Pakistan. He's seen my lifestyle, my father; his family was working in a very big company and we had this big property and we had this financial situation very well. Then when we broke down, he said, 'Okay. I'll work in [fast food chain]'.

Emma: Are you proud of him for that?

Hasan: Really, I feel very proud for my kids that the way they supported me when – when I took a job as a cleaner. He [his son] said to me, 'Papa, you don't work. I'll manage'. I said, 'No, I can do whatever I can do'. So I saw him working after school … two jobs he's working.

But his pride in his children's ready adaption to their new life was shadowed by the shame of seeking protection and not being able to secure his family's future. His emphasis on the words 'protection' and 'asylum' was tinged with disdain: 'We have asked some other government for help, for *protection*, for *asylum*. This guilt I have inside.'

73

The shame of seeking asylum was amplified by the fact that in Australia he and his family had to live with his wife's relatives, a situation that, coupled with his need to ask for protection, compromised his gendered role as provider and protector of his family:

> 'So, see, we have this culture; it was very difficult for me to dilute that I have to come and stay with my in-laws because we have this culture in Pakistan, we don't take any help from anybody. We don't live with my in-laws or we don't take any help from them.'

He attributed his discomfort to Pakistani culture, but relying on his wife's parents also hurt his sense of middle-class manhood. Hasan appealed to principles that resemble the 'householder' as an ideal category of South Asian masculinity. In their study of how migration plays into ideals of manhood in South India, anthroplogists Filippo Osella and Caroline Osella describe this category as the 'successful, social, mature man: a head of a household, holding substantial personal wealth, supporting many dependents and helping many clients' (2000: 118). At the same time, Hasan was flexible and adaptable to the demands of his new situation – he had come to terms with relinquishing his role as the exclusive economic provider for the family in a country where 'everybody has to work'.

Hasan had initially been reluctant to apply for asylum because it felt like he was forgoing his responsibility to protect his family at the same time as risking their safety. He described the decision to finally apply as sacrificing his ego for his family: 'So I thought, "I am being selfish". So why don't I just put my ego aside and live this life for my family now.' What he had to do for the sake of his family compromised his sense of self, which he repeatedly described as a sacrifice – 'I'm living for my family now'. Hasan was also confronted with the limits of his capacity to shape his own life, expressed as a sense of powerlessness:

> 'Now when my son or my daughter they ask me what is going to happen now, next; what is the state now the government has refused us to give us this – they have refused. ... So I tell them, "You just don't worry about anything. Leave everything on my shoulder. I am here". So there's nothing I can do. I cannot go and fight or anything. I can just request humbly can you please help and protect my family. That's about it.'

The ability to secure his family's future was beyond his control, his responsibility to protect them entrusted to a foreign government.

Hasan's story poured out of him during our first interview – compulsive, insistent, at times scattered. His story was both a justification and a plea:

'If you think that I'm a sinner just throw me in the ocean, just send me to a detention centre. Send me anywhere. Send me to a prison, just please for the sake of God, for the sake of Jesus you believe. Whatever religion you believe, just save my family, that's about it. That's what we want. We don't want your charity. We don't want anything from you. Just I need a protection for my kids and my wife. That's about it. That's what we want. I cannot – I don't – I don't have a lion heart to tell my family that the government is refusing us and they are sending us back.'

Hasan was expressing his desperation and his awareness of the public rhetoric about asylum-seekers as criminals. He also defended himself against the unspoken implication that he was looking for an easy life by seeking asylum, dismissively lumping social security and other forms of welfare and charity together: 'I don't want Centrelink or any of this blah, blah. We're not these kind of people who believe in living on charities or welfare. We believe in hard work. From my very young age I am a self-made man.'

In his former life in Pakistan, Hasan had been deeply involved in the informal charitable activities associated with his sect. They would provide white goods and dowries to poor families in the neighbourhood, and organise food relief for neighbourhoods devastated by bombings. Much of the charitable and philanthropic activity that takes place in Pakistan is intertwined with religious beliefs and practices, particularly Islam. There are many forms of charitable giving in Islam that 'aim to purify wealth, better the self, and improve chances of attaining paradise in the afterlife' (Kirmani and Zaidi, 2010: 19). Moving from this context to finding himself in the position where he was asking for rather than offering help felt degrading to Hasan.

The family had been told about support to help meet the basic requirements of daily life, but Hasan vehemently refused. As an asylum seeker Hasan was not eligible for social security. At the time he could have applied for the Status Resolution Support Services (SRSS) payment amounting to 89% of the unemployment benefit, though would likely have been denied because he was working. Now he would be automatically ineligible regardless of his employment status because his visa granted work rights (van Kooy and Ward, 2019). When I asked him if anyone had provided practical help, he quickly and emphatically dismissed the possibility:

'No. No. We never went to – we had this option of going to – we were told by a lot of people that, "Why don't you go to Red Cross and go to different community? They'll help you". I said, "No".'

He had a strong emotional response to any suggestion that he should seek support for day-to-day living, which he associated with begging. He would only seek support for his asylum case. Hasan told me about a fierce and upsetting argument he had had with his wife and son where they urged him to get help from one of the charity or community welfare organisations they had been told about, but he stubbornly rejected it as an option. Despite the tension and anguish it created in the family, he remained steadfast in his refusal in an effort to preserve his already damaged dignity. Hasan's unwillingness to seek or accept financial or material aid was not simply a remnant of his class and religious background in Pakistan; it also related to the dependency that seeking asylum imposed on him in a country that branded asylum seeking as criminal and parasitic.

I caught up with Hasan a few times after our original interview. He called to tell me when his hearing before the Refugee Review Tribunal was approaching, and again, when he received news that he and his family had been granted protection and Permanent Residence. If his refusal to accept charity was previously a source of tension in the family, it was now solidified as a source of pride. Hasan proudly repeated the comments of the immigration official reviewing his case: he was impressed by the strength of the family to stick together, that they had all worked to contribute to keeping the family afloat, and that Hasan had even managed to donate to charities despite his own precarious situation. The first I heard of these donations was when he told me he presented the receipts during his hearing. The official's comments were proof of the conviction Hasan held on to even at his most desperate that, if given the chance, his family could survive and thrive in Australia.

Monica's story

> 'I want to be someone who takes responsibility for my own choices and therefore is in control of my own success.'

When I first interviewed Monica she was 30, a single parent, and relied on Centrelink benefits as her only source of income. Monica was moved from Parenting Payment (Single) to the unemployment benefit (NSA) when her child turned eight, paid at a lower rate and conditional on job search requirements. She was on a break from completing her Year 12 Certificate at TAFE[1]. Monica had had a 'harsh upbringing', living first with her distant, authoritarian father, and later, with her drug-addicted, mentally unstable mother when her father gave up custody of her and her siblings. Soon after moving in with her mother she dropped out of school:

> 'I was in a refuge when I was 16. I moved out when I was 15 and then in a refuge and then – I just felt like I was on my own from a pretty

young age. Even when I lived with my parents we were still on our own in a way.'

She became pregnant at 18 and said of the early years of her daughter's life, 'I wasn't stable then, I was in bad relationships, there was a lot of things went on'. Monica had been on welfare and a daily pot (marijuana) smoker since before her daughter was born.

When I asked her about her family she told me, 'we haven't really been taught much of the stability thing and how to manage your life well. And so I guess we've all made mistakes and don't get along as well as we used to'. Her adult brother was addicted to 'ice' (methamphetamines) and in trouble with the police. He'd turn up unexpectedly at her house high or needing somewhere to sleep; she'd feed him and wash his clothes. Her mother had died of a drug overdose in suspicious circumstances two years before we sat down to interview. She had had a falling out with her sister, although they still occasionally babysat each other's children.

Monica frequently returned to this enforced independence to make sense of her responsible and caring character. She had mixed feelings about her role as the crutch of the family: 'Yeah, so I've tried to be the backbone of our family a little but I too am not completely stable. ... When I was younger it was all put on me, it wasn't a choice, like I was the oldest so I was the babysitter. ... And then we grew up and I never stopped.' It hurt her that her siblings resented her as bossy and imposing: 'Yeah, I do feel like I'm really misunderstood, because, you know, I've done it out of not just responsibility and need, but out of love. And you know, I have no – like I'm not – I don't have a debt to them, I don't owe them what I do but yet it's almost like a burden to them.' She felt torn between continuing to support her siblings, whose 'lifestyle' she didn't agree with, and putting her and her daughter's life first: 'I feel really guilty. Where's the line? I don't know how to care about them all at once.'

Choice was a recurring theme when I spoke to Monica. She was deeply critical and ashamed of her marijuana addiction, which she described as a 'loser attitude'. Her self-judgement was guided by her fierce sense of integrity, 'I feel like, you know, I've got a lot of morals. ... And it's not just knowing what's right and wrong, it's choosing to act based on what's rights and wrong and choosing right'. She was proud of her strong moral values, but it meant she felt the sting of her problems as self-imposed. 'I feel like I'm more to blame than somebody who is ignorant to it all, because I'm aware and still making those choices.'

But she was also perplexed by her addiction, 'Because I don't want to smoke, I don't enjoy the feeling anymore. ... Like, I enjoy nothing about it and yet I do it everyday. I don't get it'. She was highly reflexive about choice and its limits. She couldn't make sense of her strong desire to stop using drugs but her seeming inability to do so; she understood her addiction as her fault but not arising from rational choice. 'It's not practical, it's not responsible, and maybe that's why I'm so highly strung in every other area of my life, because that one thing I can't control.'

Monica was also ambivalent about her ambitious aspirations in the context of her long-term unemployment. She had very high standards for her moral conduct and her ambitions, but was dismissive of her achievements; she was proud of surviving but not satisfied:

> 'I have high expectations of myself but standards that I'll never reach, and I think that I might do that on purpose so that I can constantly feel, you know, not quite good enough. Like, no matter what I ever do – I could do better than that. So I don't know, maybe that's my driving coping mechanism. I don't know, like my way of excelling ever.'

She had had jobs on and off. She explained her failure to hold down a job as a case of self-sabotage:

> 'I think it's deeper than me just choosing "I don't like work!" That's not how I am; I actually do really miss it sometimes. But then I get scared of getting into it – there's this responsibility and I don't want to let anyone down. As soon as I'm actually in a job I start thinking of how I can get out of it ... but why would I get into a situation just to try and get out of it? That's really stupid.'

She speculated that it was 'laziness', or not wanting to be told what to do, but added that she's a 'good worker'. She applies herself, but 'gets bored of the same': 'So you can only clean one bathroom so well so many times and then be over it. And money's not enough of a motivation for me to go, "oh well, I'll be making the money".' Her last job was sitting inside a 2 x 1 metre display counter selling phone accessories in a shopping mall.

When I asked Monica whether unemployed people should be expected to take any job offered to them, she replied:

> 'I get it, I get it because what right do I have to say "no" to that job and then allow Centrelink and all the taxpayers to pay for my life? But I don't want to work for a fast food chain where it's killing people every day. ... Like, I want to do something that I want to do. And you know, is that being like wah, wah? ... I don't know. I don't think it's fair, but maybe it's necessary.'

Monica repeated the view that welfare recipients live off the hard-earned income of taxpayers. She equated worth with paid work and she expected, or at least wanted, fulfilment from her job. But this left her conflicted about whether her dissatisfaction with the meaningless jobs she could access was her own failing or an unfair social imposition.

Despite the internal conflict about the cause of her problems, the explanation of *social* injustice and disadvantage tended to be buried by the script of *personal* fault and failing in Monica's narrative:

'When I first moved out of home, which was a long time ago, I had nothing and I needed help then. But in my mind 10 years from then I was in way better of a place than I am now. I was ahead, not just coping. Yes, I've coped. Yes, my daughter has had what she needed. I've got this far and I suppose to an extent it's something to be proud of, but it's nothing great. I just did it, you know, like, I didn't excel really, I just did it.'

While she acknowledged her difficult upbringing as a setback, she rejected it as an 'excuse' for the limited horizons of her life. She was not satisfied with merely surviving; it was something she simply did as a matter of fact and necessity. She wanted to excel. The pride of being a good parent and the pillar of the family wasn't enough to sooth the shame of not fulfilling her ambitions in the sphere of paid work.

Monica was so aware of potential judgement that she retreated from public, anticipating even the awareness that she had been seen to cause her pain: 'Even just people seeing me, I don't even want to know that they saw me.' She avoided encounters where she expected to be judged; she stayed in the car when she picked her daughter up from school, deliberately arriving 10 minutes late so 'there's no bumping into people'. She also avoided the shops. When I asked her, 'What are you avoiding do you think?' she replied, 'Judgement, just judgement really, having to justify why I'm doing nothing, why I'm doing crap, like why I'm suffering in my relationships, why they're not going so well'.

Not long after our initial interview, Monica began casual work in a bakery franchise. Her job was to rise in the early, dark hours of the morning to ice and decorate the cakes and then organise the display at the counter. She described her manager as belittling and controlling, and was self-conscious of being the oldest among the floor staff dominated by teenagers, but she enjoyed her new work. She took pride in the care and skill she applied to decorating and displaying the cakes, despite there being little room for creativity, and it allowed her to be home in time to send her daughter off to school.

The significance of shame

Shame is a familiar theme in stories told by and about people who live disadvantage in its many forms. The pain expressed by Hasan and Monica over their perceived failings shows yet again that it is not just a shortage of material resources and power that takes a toll on the hard-done-by; it is also the more insidious erosion of self-worth and self-respect (Sennett, 2003). As theorists of recognition highlight, having our contribution and achievement disregarded by others with the same values and goals makes it harder to have a positive sense of ourselves (Honneth, 1995; Fraser and Honneth, 2003). And without a sense of self-worth and achievement it's harder to feel like there is a point pursuing our goals, which hampers our ability to take action in shaping our own life (Anderson and Honneth, 2005: 131).

The undermining effects of shame are reported in research on lived experiences of welfare and poverty that tell of humiliating encounters with welfare providers and feelings of inadequacy (Chase and Walker, 2013; Peterie et al, 2019). Health and psychology research demonstrates that welfare recipients are much more likely to experience poor mental health than people who don't receive payments, including 'significantly elevated rates of hopelessness, worthlessness and dissatisfaction with life' (Butterworth, 2008: 17). Cross-national comparative research even claims that prevalent and damaging feelings of shame are a universal feature of poverty across extremely different cultural and economic settings (Walker et al, 2013).

But while welfare stigma may be widespread, not everyone feels shame to the same degree or in the same ways. Welfare recipients who equate worth with individual ability and paid work are more prone to the negative effects of welfare stigma (Peterie et al, 2019). Welfare recipients living in working- and middle-class communities are more likely to be exposed to shame than those who live among people in a similar situation to themselves (McCormack, 2004). People find ways of coping with shame by positioning themselves as different from typical welfare recipients, rejecting personal blame by insisting on the unfairness of society or upholding alternative markers of success such as fairness or care (Davis and Hagen, 1996; Shildrick and MacDonald, 2013). Welfare stigma may be pervasive, but its effect and reach depend on the social make-up and cultural outlook of the communities stigmatised individuals move in. This point is critical for an understanding of welfare shame that is sensitive to cultural diversity (Mitchell and Vincent, 2021).

These familiar insights ring true in Monica and Hasan's accounts of their situation. Monica implied that accepting her own flawed character set her apart from other so-called 'dole bludgers', but also made her more at fault for failing to change. Hasan distanced himself from the implication that idleness or poor choices had led his family to fall on hard times by insisting 'we believe in hard work' and 'we're not these kind of people'. Hasan emphasised his personal effort to improve his situation while Monica doubted her own, yet both appealed to the idea that individuals make their own fortune. Importantly, Hasan and Monica's stories show that welfare stigma can bring about contradictory responses of pushing back against and taking on shame. This suggests the need for an approach to understanding shame that is sensitive to diversity at the level of the individual, and not simply within or across social groups.

Two familiar and dominant storylines emerge when we read Hasan and Monica's stories alongside existing academic accounts of inequality (both empirical and theoretical). Shame appears as both devastating and activating the power to act. In philosopher Axel Honneth's theory of recognition, for example, shame is a damaging symptom of disrespect, but it can also trigger social struggle by alerting individuals to their denigration (Honneth, 1995: 135, 136). According to Walker and his colleagues (2013: 230), the shame associated with poverty creates 'a sense of powerlessness' but surviving poverty still requires 'skills, inventiveness and fortitude'. These two storylines suggest the differential effects of shame and capacities to shape life in hardship. Pausing to think about how shame works and how the power to act takes different forms helps clarify the significance of shame in lived experiences of welfare.

The concept of shame is often not unpacked or fleshed out in welfare research and tends to carry the everyday meaning of negative or hindering feeling. Theories of shame, on the other hand, note its productive side (Strong, 2021). Shame makes us aware of ourselves and of our relationship to others. Shame drives us to act in particular ways – not just when it is felt, but also when it is avoided. Shame feels intimately personal; our bodies register and react to shame, creating a visceral self-consciousness. But shame is also deeply social; it depends on our awareness of and interest in others. The feeling of discomfort or pain can linger in the body and influence our sense of who we are long after the trigger has passed. Shame does not merely inhibit but also shapes our idea of who we are and how we act. Given shame's association with identity, the experience and significance of shame depends on cultural ideas of the self – the extent to which identity is felt to be stable and individual or prioritises relationship to others (Wong and Tsai, 2007).

The paralysing and productive effects of shame become clearer still when we unpack the different ways and extent to which people with relatively little power can shape their own lives. The counterpoint is the wider conditions outside of someone's control that shape their life. When researchers talk about human agency, they are concerned about how people can *make things happen* rather than simply how things *happen to them*. The sticking point is what exactly those things consist of.

For example, some have made the distinction between being able to recognise and respond to received ways of seeing and behaving versus the capacity to imagine new and different possibilities and pursue one's own projects (Emirbayer and Mische, 1998; Ortner, 2001). This is sometimes explained as the room to move within the rules of the game versus the capacity to define or change those rules. Agency is conventionally understood as deliberate and thought-out actions and choices. But humans also act in ways that are impulsive and spontaneous (Hoggett, 2000, 2001). Accounting for passionate action is important for understanding the impact of shame. Of course, in lived life these aspects of action are messy and bound together, but breaking them down into pieces helps us be clear about what we mean when we talk about the capacity to shape one's own life.

When I first spoke to Hasan and Monica, both were in situations that confronted them with the limits of free will and responsibility. Hasan and his family were terrorised in Pakistan and forced to leave their lavish life to seek asylum in Australia, where they were initially refused and awaited a review judgement. Hasan's ability to secure his family's safe future was out of his hands and under the authority of Australia's punitive immigration system. Monica, a single parent, depended on welfare to survive and was dogged by drug addiction and persistent unemployment. She was puzzled by the break between her convictions and her behaviour, and felt inadequate and disappointed in herself. They were each sick with shame about their perceived failings. Yet their shame was bound up with their efforts to recover their dignity that also produced hope, strength and pride.

Monica attributed her situation to her choices, yet they felt confusingly beyond her control. She had made bad decisions by choosing to habitually smoke pot, although she couldn't make sense of the continued hold addiction had on her – 'I enjoy nothing about it and yet I do it everyday. I don't get it.' It seemed to her like she subconsciously refused to commit to a 'meaningless' job – 'why would I get into a situation just to get out of it?' The discrepancy between her understanding of her free will and her experience of powerlessness was disconcerting. Hasan also seemed disoriented by the unfamiliar sides of himself during our first conversation. He didn't recognise himself, the person who couldn't provide for his family and had to ask a foreign government for asylum. He found himself profoundly out of place (Probyn, 2004) – in the country he was in, in his life, in himself – and it called forth aspects of himself he didn't recognise.

Trying to grasp how individuals get stuck or behave self-destructively or senselessly, Richard Hoggett (Hoggett, 2000) argues that humans aren't always familiar with the parts of themselves that their thoughts, feelings and behaviour stem from. This argument is based on the idea that we have different sides and characters that come out in different settings and moments in time. The French sociologist, Bernard Lahire (2011), proposes that this is because individuals in complex societies learn how to think and behave in many different social settings with competing conventions and cultural influences. According to this understanding of human actors, a single individual may be motivated by a range of conscious and unconscious motives that may not always be consistent. Contradictory behaviour may feel confusing and unsettling for someone who imagines themself to have a coherent identity.

Upholding cultural ideals of self-reliance and self-responsibility had both enabling and disabling aspects for Monica, although not in equivalent measure. She judged herself severely as a parasitic 'dole bludger'. Making the vitriol of public rhetoric her own meant she experienced her shame as personal and consuming (Frost and Hoggett, 2008: 445, following Goffman, 1968). She blamed herself for failing to sustain work, but saw in that personal responsibility the potential for change: 'If we say it's our fault then we can change the outcome or you can change the circumstances.' Owning her situation supported her strong sense of integrity, which she was proud of and which she felt differentiated her from her troubled family and other so-called 'dole bludgers'. Monica's faith in self-mastery gave her hope for an alternative future; it energised and motivated her. But it also meant she felt the weight of blame for not changing rested squarely on her, and the shame of it eroded her self-esteem and restricted where she would go in public.

A culture that celebrates individual ability as what sets a person apart from others strikes at the core of how they feel about themselves; even for those who know that inner ability is unevenly cultivated and acknowledged, it's hard to avoid feeling like not making it is a sign of personal weakness or inadequacy (Sennett and Cobb, 1972). Monica selectively and reflexively took up these ideas as her own by invoking the power of personal choice as a motivating mantra. And yet, holding to that logic reinvigorated its power to shame and undermine her, proving an inadequate resource for changing the situation she found herself in. Giving life to a culture of personal responsibility, then, is not synonymous with empowerment.

Like Monica, Hasan's efforts to relieve shame and recover dignity were at once self-preserving and anguished. He was proud of his family's fortitude in responding to the burdens of their circumstance, yet ashamed to have to bear those burdens. His determined refusal to accept welfare or charity, despite the financial and emotional strain the family was under, eased the shame of being in a position where he would benefit from such help. But it conflicted with his determination to put his family before his pride, creating anguish within the family and himself. He was conflicted by his responsibilities as role model, provider and protector, husband, father and son-in-law in the family, roles that suddenly felt not so easy to reconcile. But he was also able to adapt to a new worldview in which 'everybody has to work'. Insisting on donating to charity despite his own hardship, alongside his family working together, crystallised as a source of enormous pride once the family's future in Australia was secured. His declaration that he is a 'self-made man', coupled with his refusal to accept charity, was perhaps both a defence against the label 'opportunistic asylum-seeker' as well as an expression of his faith in his ability to (re)make something of himself in Australia.

Monica asserted dignity in the face of shame by embracing the power of personal choice and herself as a vehicle for change. Hasan negotiated shame by shifting from himself to his family. While he described the shame of seeking asylum as debilitating his ego, there was an implied honour in sacrificing himself to his family that was socially dignifying. He was influenced by South Asian ideals of collective family honour and the importance of prioritising it. Self-sacrifice for the success of the family and investment in children as the hope of the future is a common template of the migration trajectory. Hasan remained convinced even at his most desperate that, if his family were granted protection, they would build a successful life in Australia. His shame did not dent this conviction but rather channelled it.

While Monica had not experienced the profound uprooting that Hasan had, her understanding of herself and her circumstances was also defined by multiple and competing cultural influences – albeit less pronounced. They were evident in her disposition to care for her siblings out of love and not just obligation; the rejection of money as a motivator or measure of success; the sense of social responsibility expressed in not wanting 'to work for a fast food chain where it's killing people every day'; and her ambition to excel and find meaning in paid work. However, shifting from the self to the family did not offer Monica the same reprieve from her chronic shame as it offered Hasan. She was also proud of her enduring commitment to her siblings and the way she had raised her daughter, but it was expressed modestly and buried in the shame of unemployment. It was overshadowed by paid work as the primary reference of value.

Monica's shame was bound up with her thwarted ambition; aspiring to excel both excited and disappointed her. She seemed to have taken on board the denigrating rhetoric about 'job snobs' – unemployed (young) people who are said to aim too high but not have the skills or work ethic to match their expectations. 'I want to do something that I want to do. And you know, is that like wah, wah? I don't know. I don't think it's fair but maybe it's necessary.' She imagined 'getting ahead' but felt paralysed in the present, her template of a trajectory more tentative than Hasan's, and her conviction in its arrival more tenuous.

Imagining future paths makes it possible to react inventively to existing ways of thinking and behaving and generate new possibilities (Emirbayer and Mische, 1998: 984). People disadvantaged by inequality do not lack aspiration. Monica's intelligent and active imagination attested to this. As the anthropologist Arjun Appadurai (2004: 188) argues, the opportunities and resources to explore the future and become practised at pursuing projects are unevenly distributed. Only through experience can we know the route to where we want to go and have the confidence that we will successfully make the journey. He calls this 'the capacity to aspire'.

The difference between Monica and Hasan's 'capacity to aspire' seems be in their confidence in the possible paths they imagine and the reach of their projections, a difference that is classed and gendered. While Hasan viewed his obstacle as external – the Refugee Review Tribunal ruling – for Monica it seemed to come from within. Monica's feeling of self-sabotage – her persistent drug addiction and restlessness in menial jobs – seemed to undermine her confidence in her pursuit of her ambitions. The collective frustration of aspiration felt to Monica like personal inadequacy and failure, making the sting of it all the more painful (Sennett and Cobb, 1972).

Conclusion

The power of shame to both limit and stimulate the direction of one's life is implicit in existing literature on class inequality. The constraining power of shame is evident in its attention to the sense of worthlessness and inadequacy that disproportionately weighs on those disadvantaged by inequality. The animating power of shame is reflected in the emphasis on diverse responses to shame and the varying conditions and resources that make some people more adept to protect themselves from stereotypes and negative judgements. Making these two aspects of shame explicit allows for an account of the shame of protection that neither valorises nor dismisses the capacity of people living in difficult circumstances to shape their own lives.

By pointing to the productive side of shame, my point is not to downplay the harm that shame can inflict on people who are made to feel like their deprivation is the result of their own personal shortcomings. Economic hardship doesn't just make the practicalities of life more difficult; it also makes it harder to feel like a worthwhile person in a society that looks down on poverty as a personal failing and welfare as a 'free ride'. Even if people find ways of living with or against denigrating treatment, the burden is unfair (Anderson and Honneth, 2005: 131).

But I have avoided drawing a clear line between those who absorb shame and those who manage to repel it. Understanding the power of shame to shape and define even as it stifles and paralyses opens up a more complicated picture of the impact of shame on lived experiences of welfare. Rather than setting shame in opposition to dignity, reading Monica and Hasan's stories closely shows how the anticipation and experience of shame is entangled with efforts to maintain and recover dignity.

7

The art of getting by

Greg, an Anglo man in his 60s, shoplifted daily. After a trip to the supermarket, Greg would neatly lay out his illicit haul on the kitchen table before stowing it away for future use. His mischievous smile told me he was showing off as well as taking stock. He only stole from the big corporate supermarkets, he assured me, never small businesses. He'd recently curbed his activity when he had been caught and banned from the supermarket. Greg had come of age during the counter-culture of the 1960s and 1970s, and had rejected the Protestant work ethic of his lower middle-class parents. He had shifted between family and unemployment benefits for the best part of three decades, interspersed with short stints of cash-in-hand work since he lost his full-time administrative job almost 30 years ago. When we met, he had recently moved on to the comparatively more generous Age Pension and had been relieved of the job search requirements attached to unemployment benefits.

Much of what Greg shoplifted was not strictly necessary for getting by. He accumulated expensive toiletries which he regularly brought home as offerings for his wife. He stole moisturiser, socks and underwear to gift on birthdays and Christmas. Greg's home displayed the clutter of a compulsive collector. He proudly showed off his DVDs while his wife complained he never watched them. Piles of second-hand books lined the walls and dated magazines over-flowed from cardboard boxes. Greg regularly stole small plastic figurines that he saved up to give to his nieces as a full set. He smuggled specialist magazines to present to his teenage son. His lifted gifts were imperfect gestures of care to the people he loved.

Greg's story is a striking example of the sometimes creative and surreptitious ways people find of navigating life on social security payments. It's not hard to imagine critics using Greg's story to bemoan the corrupting influence of permissive public welfare and defenders celebrating it as a heroic act of defiance. But Greg's actions defy neat classification as strategic survival, responsible caretaking or dysfunctional 'acting out' that often seems to characterise accounts of poor people's actions. His lifted gifts illustrate something more modest but nonetheless important. They are tokens of luxury and gestures of affection for his family. Gifts – whether they are objects or actions – play an important social role in affirming and sustaining relationships (Komter, 2005). Greg's lifted gifts enabled him to participate in this social exchange even when money was scarce. They gave him a sense of purpose, pleasure and accomplishment that made a liveable life in poverty possible.

More than making do

Les Back (2015: 832) – a sociologist of working-class culture and everyday life – has argued that sociological stories of 'damage, hopelessness and injustice' are compelling but crowd out 'moments of the repair and hope in which a livable life is made possible'. Unangax̂[1] scholar Eve Tuck (2009) also points to the cost of imagining marginalised communities as invariably damaged and depleted when research is driven by a strategy of documenting harm and injury in order to achieve reparation. She advocates desire as an alternative research frame: 'Desire, yes, accounts for the loss and despair, but also the hope, the visions, the wisdom of lived lives and communities' (Tuck, 2009: 417).

This chapter focuses on the moments of hope and repair embedded in ways of getting by in hardship. But focusing on hope instead of damage is also fraught given that the ideal of resilience comes with expectations that people thrive through a life of insecurity (Donoghue and Edmiston, 2020: 14). We must not underestimate the cultural appeal of stories about people who, against all odds, refuse to let their circumstances get them down. Too often the label 'deserving' is reserved for welfare users deemed to display the right blend of misfortune and fortitude. Those who struggle to cope are exposed to accusations of incompetence or blame. The challenge is to tell of hope amid the strain of life on welfare without falling into overly rosy accounts of resilience or reinforcing the expectation that people face difficult situations with plucky resolve.

Since the 1990s, welfare researchers have paid increasing attention to the possibility embedded in welfare users' capacity to manage and impact difficult situations both created and mitigated by social policy. Attention turned to the routines, skills, materials and networks that allow some people to cope with adversity relatively unscathed compared to others. This shift in emphasis reflected a search for more nuanced explanations of the impact of adverse circumstances, which could account for an individual's capacity to shape their own lives as well as forces beyond their control. Researchers were also looking to write about life on welfare in a way that promoted dignity and challenged assumptions of passivity and dependence. While this shift has been broadly embraced, it has also been charged with producing naively optimistic accounts of the resistant and resilient capacities of individuals (for a discussion of this literature, see Lister, 2015; Mitchell, 2022).

Literature on lived experiences of welfare also tends to be reactive in orientation (see Mitchell, 2022). By this I mean it's focused on how people respond to threats to their welfare and make do in situations often beyond their control. Even the stuff that gives life meaning – identity, belonging, relationships – is framed as a strengthening asset against adversity. This reactive emphasis makes sense in policy-oriented research that seeks to understand how people deal with hardship and how systems of informal and formal social support affect their capacity to do so.

But focusing on reactive forms of adaptation and refusal risks burying the projects and desires that give people meaning and purpose outside of their relationship to the welfare system. Instead, I want to draw attention to the pleasures, pursuits and values that nourish and sustain life, even in hardship. This chapter offers a hopeful and pragmatic outlook, but not necessarily on a grand scale. Lived lives are complex and ambiguous, and not all ways of getting by fit comfortably with ideas of 'good resilience' or function simply as a means to an end. The aim is to do justice to the moments that enrich difficult lives without romanticising or ennobling them.

Everyday care and accomplishment

Almost everyone I spoke to was 'counting coins'. Some felt the pinch of stretching an income made up at least in part by support payments. For others, meeting the cost of living was a daily struggle. When I asked how they got by on very little income they described the practicalities of budgeting, rationing, prioritising rent or urgent repairs, putting off paying bills, borrowing money from family, getting food or amenities vouchers from welfare organisations or charities or going without – from leaving ginger out of the curry or living on spaghetti on toast to skipping meals. Their responses echoed the picture of actively 'juggling, piecing together and going without' (Lister, 2004: 133) found in other studies of life on income support payments.

Getting by is, by definition, geared towards dealing with a situation where something is lacking. But ways of getting by can also be more than a means to an end. Helen Holmes (2019) recently made this point about thrift, showing how it is motivated by conscience about waste and enjoyment of ingenuity as well as financial necessity. Similarly, I found that ways of getting by could also be ways of affirming relationships with family, friends and community by showing care. They could give people a sense of purpose and achievement. But I had to look carefully to recognise the value embedded in the mundane practices that amounted to more than the practical sum of their parts.

'Just being there'

'Just being there' was a common answer when I asked what makes a supportive family. At first, I took this as a cursory response. Perhaps I needed to rephrase my questions to draw out more substantial answers, I thought. When I pressed people for examples from their own family, the kinds of things that came to mind were often so modest and mundane they seemed inconsequential or predictable. Eli, a young man, told me how his brother would make him toast when he returned home from hospital. Leena's father would deliberately buy too many veggies and drop some round to his adult daughters and, even though they insisted they were 'big girls now', they were touched by the gesture. Every week the elderly volunteers at the church playgroup would send Bill home with his favourite cheese and pickle sandwiches – a welcome treat given his daily struggle to put food on the table.

'Just being there' seemed to be about sharing time and company as much as implying reliability. Dropping in or hosting drop-ins for a cuppa was routine for Greg and Monica, who had both been unemployed for more of their adult life than not. They passed time trading in banter and gossip, sometimes asking for or offering a loan or favour – the trade agreements written in instant coffee. There was value in passing time together without pretences. As one member of a supported Aboriginal group explained:

> 'It's like everybody is *equal* here. Like, it's not, "you're better than me or I've got more money than you". It's like – this is gonna sound bad – we're all *Black*, and we're all cut from the same piece of cloth. We're all equal. We're not talking about, "Aw, I've got this mortgage, and you know, I've just bought this car, I just did this".'

The group allowed them to spend time with people who shared their simple tastes and mores – people who were 'happy to sit out the front with toast and a ciggie'.

'Being there' is something that welfare organisations deliberately cultivate by investing in community development. But, at least among the members I spoke to, the group was seen as organic rather than orchestrated. As Ronda put it, 'It is our group. I don't see it as a service'. Another member of the supported Aboriginal group suggested that opportunities to get together were particularly important in suburban Sydney where Aboriginal relatives and friends were dispersed:

> 'I come from a town where it's all Aboriginal people there. So everyone's all in close together. But here there isn't any area like that where there's just all Aboriginal people in one spot. It's not the same feeling for me here as it is back there. … Yeah, so it's just – it's been a great group bringing all the Aboriginal people, families together.'

Kane and Nessa echoed this sentiment when they described an annual event funded by a local community organisation, laughing as they said, 'We never seen so many Black Kids out here!', 'It's like finally seeing Black kids'. This shows how locally based community organisations play a role in linking up Aboriginal residents beyond kin in suburban Sydney (Yamanouchi, 2010).

During my fieldwork I attended a number of supported community events and family programmes where I met many of my interviewees. Reem, a young single mother, valued the routine afforded by the scheduled playgroup I met her at: 'Makes you look forward to the day, you know. It's nice to just stop worrying about things and just come and relax and meet other people and get together and have fun and talk.' She would volunteer to chop the fruit as a way of reciprocating, even though she couldn't contribute financially. For Reem and others I spoke to, the group provided an outlet for their children to learn and play when there wasn't enough money for outings. Nadira had arrived in Australia only a year ago with her young family. She had found it difficult to adjust to the loss of status and family support, not to mention the cost of living. The local public activities she actively sought out allowed her to meet new people and learn about local customs, providing an entry point to the local community. Even the most banal and intangible practices that foster resilience occur in informal or semi-formal spaces that need investment rather than the withdrawal of ongoing State support (Andres and Round, 2015).

Rather than being cursory or insignificant, then, 'just being there' can be understood as a form of 'social repair' (Thrift, 2005; Hall and Smith, 2015). Urban geographers use this term to capture the mundane and minute practices of care and upkeep that produce and nurture social relationships. The concept understands 'unremarked, everyday resilience' (Hall and Smith, 2015: 3) as regenerative rather than simply reactive. Just as the physical infrastructure of the city is continually regenerated through repair and maintenance work, 'just being there' is part of the quiet bustle of activity that regenerates a meaningful and liveable social life (Thrift, 2005: 136). 'Just being there' is intimate and informal; it involves caring in the most routine and banal ways. It nourishes the relationships that are drawn on in hard times. It also makes for moments of pleasure and purpose in their own right.

Of course, 'just being there' isn't all rosy. Optimism about the sustenance derived from informal relationships is tempered by the inadequacy of private support for many of the most in need and the strain that looking after friends and family places on women especially (Harrison, 2012; Offer, 2012). Many of the people I spoke to were dealing with addiction or mental illness in the family – sometimes both. Some felt there was no option but to be there because there was no alternative. For example, Monica continued to wash her homeless brother's clothes, no matter how badly he mistreated her as he descended further into his 'ice' (methamphetamine) addiction. She described her caring nature as a strength, but still felt that he took it for granted that she would be there for him, no matter what. He certainly did not return the favour. For Monica, the burden of being there was unevenly carried and made all the heavier by the absence of outside support.

On top of that, the motives and effects of care are not necessarily benevolent. Hall and Smith (2015: 14) make this point when they insist that 'social repair' is different to physical repair because the caring activities that fuel social life involve power and reciprocity. Care may be offered selfishly, it may be unwanted, or bestowed on terms that are not the recipient's own. Nadira sensed this when the Lebanese-Muslim owners of the property she rented visited every day during Ramadan, despite having never made the effort before. She explained: 'I feel that maybe they think that we are so much poor and that's why they are coming, so it made me feel really, really bad. Maybe she was doing it for her good, she thought that maybe she would get some good deeds from going, but it was not good for me.'

Nessa, a young single mother with welfare as her only source of income, felt it too when she rejected the invitation to change by attending a supported playgroup as a condition of receiving housing. She considered it a patronising waste of time and a blatant discredit to her job as a parent: 'I was like "Nah, I'm a grown-arse woman, I don't need people watching me".' Acknowledging the conflicted nature of both informal and formal care is necessary if we are to avoid idealising the pleasure and sustenance it may offer.

'We like to look after each other'

Focusing on ways of getting by as a reaction to difficult circumstances risks burying the cultural orientations brought to life through making do. Much of what is written about resilience positions cultural ties and social relationships as strengthening 'resources' or 'assets' within families or communities (Seccombe, 2002; Orthner et al, 2004). This recognises how cultural identity and belonging may equip people to deal with hardships and endure despite them. Of course, cultural and social connection can be both a self-affirmation of identity and empowerment and a reaction to outside pressures and impositions. But this may be missed when a resilience framework subsumes the pursuits that give life meaning and value in its responsive outlook. It is perhaps all the more important, then, to look beyond a reactive lens in order to do justice to cultural diversity.

Almost all of the people I spoke to valued family support, but some talked about it as a cultural orientation and category of value. People from migrant backgrounds where English is not the main language and Aboriginal backgrounds sometimes referred to family relations in ethno-cultural terms in a way that Anglo-Australian participants did not, at times implying that it set them apart from 'typical Australians'. Previous research has also found that Anglo-Australians tend to perceive their values and practices of caring as 'culture-free' while non-Anglo-Australians are more aware of being part of a 'non-normative culture' (Cardona et al, 2006: 16, 43). The boundaries between generative and reactive forms of cultural expression may be blurred for those who inhabit non-normative and marginalised cultures.

The strength of family support as a cultural orientation recurred particularly in my interview with Leena and Samah, sisters born in Australia to a Muslim-Lebanese father and Anglo mother who converted to Islam. Both were mothers themselves. They continually made comparisons between the Arab and Anglo sides of the extended family, as well as between their husbands – Leena's born and raised in Lebanon and Samah's an Anglo-Australian. They took pride in their 'family-oriented' Arab sensibility and the less 'judgmental' outlook they saw as inherited from their Anglo side, proudly describing themselves as 'multicultural' and 'half-half ethnic'. Leena affectionately boasted about the closeness of her adult siblings and parents, revolving particularly around her father:

'Yeah, money wise, if I need money at the shops and I'm pretty tight, and mum's with me, she'll give me money. Dad will give money. … He still has to look after his kids. My brother bought his own house and all in one go his roof collapsed, his hot water system went, his this and that. So my dad, of course, was there – my dad is very handy, he helps us every time we move.'

Samah confirmed her sister's description: 'You can't go to my dad's house without taking something home.'

Leena talked about her husband's giving character as a source of both pride and tension in their marriage: 'It caused us a bit of dramas; he can't say no to anyone. He's the type – he'll drop everything and help someone. [But] Dude you have a wife and kids, I understand you like helping people but then we were last.' She was similarly equivocal about his shouldering the burden of support for his family back in Lebanon: 'He cops all the burden overseas but we support them and thank god we can, because we're lucky here we can support them. … Well, some [of his siblings] get greedy, when they come here there's some that want to take a lot, they think we're from Australia, we're rich.' Despite shifting between expressions of pride and frustration, being culturally 'family-oriented' was a defining characteristic in Leena and Samah's narrative about everyday life. It was a major source of identity, not to mention everyday occupation and enjoyment.

Adrian was deeply proud to belong to an extended Aboriginal family. He told me how his family 'like to look after each other', which he explained in terms of respect: 'Respect has a lot to do with it. It comes from our grandparents. They learned their kids to respect their elders and so forth down the line until my parents learned me about respecting my elders, and I'm doing the same with my kids.' At celebrations 'everyone puts a bit of money to make it as special as could be'. He told me how when a relative died the extended family banded together to help cover the cost of the funeral and make sure everyone got there:

> 'The aunties got on the phone to let everyone know. We all chipped in to help hire a bus or something from that town, pay for petrol, pay for food, make sure everyone got there. ... We all just chipped in what we could and we got the money together to help pay for the funeral.'

Adrian put into words how everyday care affirms family ties: 'we all come together as a family and we showed each other what we meant to each other'. Contributing is not simply an implied obligation but creates the bonds that give that obligation meaning.

While this could be taken as a generic description of family life, in this case it speaks to the cultural distinctiveness of Aboriginal modes of relating in which kin relationships are integral to Aboriginal identity. This is often expressed in terms of 'caring and sharing' as a form of social obligation that maintains kin relationships and a sense of 'self-in-relationship' (MacDonald, 2000: 97). This example is clearly not reducible to the responsive capacity to manage an unexpected and costly funeral. Rather, it shows how ways of getting by can also regenerate cultural practices and ties – in this case affirming relationships by being available to fulfil the needs of family members.

In contrast to Adrian, Bill repeatedly expressed the burden of family expectations as a tension between Aboriginal culture of 'everyone helps everyone' and individual aspirations:

> 'Because in Aboriginal culture say if you've got a car, well, that's everyone's car. But over the years things change and just because you go to work and you struggle to save and you buy yourself a nice house and you set yourself up, well, you just can't say to the mob come on, put tents up in the back yard fellas. Those days are gone.'

The tensions that unequal changes in income and employment status introduce to Aboriginal modes of family obligation is a recurring theme in ethnographies of Aboriginal social relationships (MacDonald, 2000; Gibson, 2010; Cowlishaw, 2011). Bill told me about his brother coming to him and expecting money or the use of his car, but he was ambiguous about whether this was a personal or cultural trait: 'I think he was just using you up. He didn't like to go to work and he expected the family to support him. That was all it was.' Bill's frustration reminds us that Aboriginal practices of 'caring and sharing' may also be conflicted and complicated.

Whether culturally distinct forms of obligation are considered valuable assets in the face of poverty depends on who is looking and what they expect to find. Aboriginal forms of 'caring and sharing' have been framed as both a strength to be harnessed and as a weakness to be targeted in recent policy approaches (Altman, 2011). Those in favour of restricting how Aboriginal welfare recipients spend their payments have argued that 'passive welfare' has turned demand sharing – a form of giving initiated by the request of the receiver without the expectation of return – from a 'valuable cultural tradition' into a dysfunctional form of Aboriginal culture (Pearson, 2007; Altman, 2011: 195–6). Opponents argue that it is cultural strength that has allowed Aboriginal families and communities to endure generations of dysfunctional government policy and the trauma and poverty left in its wake (Brough et al, 2004). From this standpoint, affirming family ties and cultural identities is both self-determining *and* resistant in a context where Indigenous culture and family life has long been scrutinised and controlled.

'We know how to extend the dollar'

Many of the people I spoke to counted coins begrudgingly, but for a few, efficient budgeting was a source of considerable pride. Their diligence with money conformed to what outsiders looking in might expect resourcefulness to look like. Talk of 'managing' hardship can be a way of distancing oneself from the tainted image of welfare recipients as incapable and irresponsible or denying that one is poor (Shildrick et al, 2012: 289). Many of the people I spoke to certainly rejected the label of poverty regardless of how deep or drawn-out their hardship was. The few who vocally took pride in managing well talked about their ability to 'extend the dollar' as an accomplishment that signalled their good character and set them apart from others. They may have implicitly positioned themselves as 'deserving' of welfare by upholding the capacity to get by, but it was others who needed riches to be satisfied with life that were the explicit counterpoint to their humble self-image.

Ronda became a mother in her teens. She described a long history of scraping through and difficult times, but insisted, 'We've lived on a small income, but we've worked out how to get by'. She described the breakdown of her budget in detail, telling me how much came out for power and phone bills and was automatically debited for rent. She boasted about her capacity to be strict on herself and her children when it came to spending money:

Emma: How are things now?
Ronda: Really good! [enthusiastic] I mean, we are in
           Aboriginal Housing, but we own two cars. We don't

have any [outstanding] bills because I'm so strict on myself for budgeting, I literally allow myself $30 a day, $30 and that's it. You know, if we need something else – sorry – that's my budget for the day. We don't go over that budget. I mean, I'll do a food shop and then after the food shop that's my budget – $30 and that's it.

When I questioned whether that was easy to stick to with the children, she said she used it to instil the same skill in her sons by rewarding them at the end of the fortnight with a treat. Ronda had taught her eight-year-old to save his modest allowance every week. She boasted that he had refused to let her buy him new shoes:

'He's like, "No, I wanna have enough money in my bank so I can pay for my own shoes". And he's only got about $65/just on $70 … and 'cos he only wears Nikes his shoes are $80 at the moment. And so I said, "just take the money out and mum will pay the rest". [He replies] "No, mum, I wanna pay it." Because he's earn't that money and he's been saving that money … I mean it's been taking him weeks, but he just won't budge on us.'

She went on to tell me about her 17-year-old: 'He's like, "Mum, I need new shoes" and I'm like, "You get money so you do it. If your brother can save, you can save." [She says with pride] And then he rings up last night, "mum, I bought a new pair of shoes today".'

Thriftiness was a value borne out of the necessity of raising a family on a meagre income, but it was a skill Ronda had mastered and a principle she was proud to instil in her children. It was linked to the standards of discipline and care that were closely intertwined for Ronda, who saw her job as a mother to prepare her children to survive in a tough world.

For the few people I spoke to who upheld budgeting as a principle, it was more than a practical way of making ends meet in the present; it was used to invoke humble family origins and values. Aisha was a Lebanese-Australian stay-at-home mother. Her husband's income was supplemented by her family benefits:

'We're pretty smart, me and my husband. … We know how to extend the dollar. I've come from a very humble family. We never had an extravagant life. I'm used to living on the minimum, so to me it didn't really bother me, to me I didn't feel it. To me, it's a shelter over my head, I'm eating, I'm with the man I love, so it's nothing I care about.'

She conceded that it wasn't always easy: 'But don't get me wrong, there were times where it was a bit tough; things you wanted but you couldn't really get. But we still managed to save enough to have our holiday every year. It was nice.' Aisha, like Ronda, defined success in terms of principles of discipline and care, and these principles were embedded in budgeting as a way of getting by. As Michèle Lamont (2000: 4) puts it, these principles 'function as an alternative to economic definitions of success and offer a way to maintain dignity and to make sense of their lives'.

However, Aisha's qualification – 'don't get me wrong' – offers an important caveat. Both she and Ronda had young children and an income from their husbands' work that shielded them somewhat from the stigma of being mothers on welfare, and allowed them some leeway to budget for comforts like new trainers or holidays. Some of the people I interviewed described surviving on welfare payments as a constant struggle to juggle the cost of bills, rent and food, let alone unexpected expenditure such as school excursions, medication or specialist appointments. Consistent with other research (Dwyer, 2000; Murphy et al, 2011), the first thing people surviving on welfare would mention missing out on was often socialising, treats, outings or holidays – 'you can't do nothing with your kids', as Kane put it. Thriftiness and self-discipline offered little comfort to people barely getting by, and worn down by the effort.

'Sometimes it's not worth it'

Not all the practices I encountered sat so comfortably within normative ideas of 'good' resilience, even if they were motivated by similar principles of care and maintenance as some of the more conventional ways of getting by. As Elizabeth Harrison (2012: 104) argues, expecting resilience to manifest in normative terms 'does not do justice to the ways [people] do in fact get by'. Nor does it acknowledge how ways of getting by may have value beyond making ends meet.

There was a quiet satisfaction in Dylan's detailed description of foraging at the rubbish dump for copper wire and aluminium cans to sell as scrap metal. He was a single father, Anglo, in his 30s, and living with his young son at his parents' house when I spoke with him. He was looking for work and living off the Parenting Payment (PP) with the begrudging help of his parents. He had struggled with alcohol addiction in the recent past, and still smoked pot daily like his girlfriend, Monica, who introduced us. Monica did not mention her visits to the dump when I first spoke to her separately. Like the women in Harrison's (2012) UK-based study, she was preoccupied with how she would ration the food to make it last for her and her daughter as well as accommodating Dylan and her brother if they happened to be hanging around at mealtime.

Dylan told me about stripping electrical wire, and that they wouldn't melt the plastic off even though it was quicker because it was worse for the environment. The price they could fetch for copper had dropped a lot so they aimed for aluminium instead; it was worth less, but it was more readily available. The hard work was far from lucrative: 'But by the time you pay the petrol [for the trip to the dump] sometimes it's not worth it. Sometimes you might go out, I think we've made 60 or 70 bucks in one day off the tip.'

Dylan explained prices, methods, pros and cons to me for quite some time, shifting between enthusiasm for the quiet pleasures to be found – 'It's like a treasure hunt really; I've found some awesome stuff' – and the fact that 'it's really just not worth it'. He told me about an old war medal he found in a drawer while Monica chimed in to show off the functional iPod they had found, a pair of good-as-new boots, and the ornaments that Monica's daughter repainted and gifted to extended family. They both marvelled at the things people throw away.

Even though the labour they invested did not pay off financially, they expressed a certain satisfaction at the initiative and energy they applied to the task and their contribution to reducing landfill:

'If I go to the tip for five hours there's five hours I haven't been smoking pot, so it's probably actually saving me money going to the tip and spending that on petrol [laughs] than smoking 50 bucks worth of pot, but um. [perks up again] I kind of, I find it fun, and even when I'm back in the workforce, now for the rest of my life I'll probably just have a few drums in my shed that I'll just continually fill them up ... Monica collected 11 kilos of cans in three hours, that's like a 44 gallon drum full of crushed cans. I don't know how she did it myself. And the amount of cans now that aren't gonna get buried have gone to be reused and recycled – I think it's a good thing ... I think in a way we've done the world a favour.'

Dylan framed the value of scrounging as a form of distraction from his drug habit and an expression of social and environmental responsibility, as well as being simply 'fun'.

Dylan's understated pride could not be confused with sentimentality. When I asked him in what situation he would find himself making a trip to the tip he replied: 'Desperation. If we've got credit from a pot dealer I need to pay it two days before pay day, we might be able to [make it from the tip].' Even so, it offered him satisfaction, pleasure and value – albeit modestly expressed – irrespective of its practical purpose or financial payoff.

The point is not to celebrate Dylan, or Greg and his lifted gifts, as heroic figures. Like all humans, Dylan and Greg were flawed; they both struggled with gambling and drug addiction, which are recognised health problems that also put emotional and financial strain on their families. While I have insisted on paying attention to the moments that make life liveable, the line between enriching and destructive pleasures and pursuits is not necessarily clear. Dylan himself was conflicted about this; he shifted between describing scrounging at the rubbish dump as a worthwhile pursuit or as a waste of time. While it's important to acknowledge the capacity to hope and not just cope in hardship, neither are inherently constructive or successful.

Living, not just surviving

I remember the moment I learned that just hanging around with my out-of-work parents was valuable in its own way. I had discovered the shame of not being 'normal' in my first year of school when I arrived late in a taxi after missing the bus (not the most efficient use of limited money, but my parents had decided I'd missed too much school already). One of my classmates was incredulous to learn my family didn't have a car. I missed a lot of school, and on my days home I would gain favour by making cuppas for the adults that dropped by, listening in on gripes and gossip. I would join my dad as he ferried loads of shopping home on foot from the supermarket on payday, taking the last bite of our pastry before we reached home so our treat wasn't discovered. When I reappeared at school after a number of days away, the same classmate – a few years older now – told me she didn't get to see her parents much. 'My mum and dad are always at work', she said sadly. I inwardly revelled in the knowledge that I had something she missed out on.

The focus on minute and muted examples of everyday care and accomplishment is perhaps all the more relevant given the limited resources at the disposal of people struggling to get by. 'Just being there' was about sharing time and company even if there was nothing else to spare. Pride in budgeting made a virtue of a necessity. Scrounging at the rubbish dump expressed diligence of a sort. And, at the more sensational end of the spectrum, perhaps, shoplifting allowed Greg to show he cared by giving gifts he otherwise couldn't afford. The tokens of luxury were relished because they were beyond the means of his family's meagre income.

Yet small pleasures can be judgementally disparaged as wasteful and imprudent in public discourse. Take a scene in the first season of *Struggle Street* (2015, 6.12 mins), a controversial television documentary about poverty in the western Sydney suburb of Mount Druitt. The cameras follow Ashley and his mate Tony as they make some extra cash from collecting and selling scrap metal. They immediately spend the $29 they make buying sandwiches and a Caesar salad from a Service Station (not the most economically efficient place to shop). 'Just a little bit of luxury we enjoy', Tony tells the camera, followed by the sanctimonious lament of the narrator: 'It's two steps forward, three steps back as this luxury feed eats up the arvo's [afternoon's] earnings'. The implication is that welfare recipients should bear missing out on treats, outings or holidays with humble determination.

Like Ashley and Tony, neither Dylan nor Greg's habits would likely be considered responsible or constructive by conventional definitions. Scrounging at the rubbish dump offered little in the way of financial payoff for Dylan, and he characterised it himself as an act of desperation. Yet it also afforded him a sense of independence and satisfaction, not to mention a welcome distraction. Greg's shoplifting was perhaps more lucrative, but the real reward was the thrill of pulling one over the corporate supermarket, the pleasure of collecting, and the ability to express his affection for his family. While occasionally such schemes may deliver material reward – some extra cash or treats that would otherwise have to be foregone – their value exceeded any practical function and sat uncomfortably with a purely instrumental account of getting by.

The more banal ways of 'just being there' may be more recognisable as a source of strength and resilience if they were not so 'ephemeral' and difficult to observe (Andres and Round, 2015: 667). As Lisa McKenzie (2015: 53) points out, strength and resilience 'are usually buried very deeply within a neighbourhood, and are often missed and discarded, especially within political, policy and media rhetoric about poor neighbourhoods'. Ways of getting by may not resemble the 'resources' or 'assets' policymakers and researchers are looking for, or may be dismissed as irresponsible or destructive. Welfare recipients are often talked *about* and expected to resemble worn-out and one-dimensional motifs of poverty and vulnerability, but resilience can be conflicted, embodying care and conflict, sustenance and strain. The line between strengthening and undermining ways of getting by is not always sharply defined.

Importantly, recognising the hopeful side of life even in hardship must not obscure how more expansive aspirations are limited by poverty. The distinction between living and merely surviving recurred among those I spoke to living in the worst hardship. Nessa, a young single mother with welfare as her only source of income, described getting by as scraping through: '[You're] Just living so basic. You're like on the poverty line – you're just surviving. You've just paid your rent, your bills, got enough for food, there's nothing else really.' However, it was not an expression of hope amid deprivation, but the deprivation of hope. One's pleasures and pursuits are certainly hampered when energy and resources are absorbed in hanging on. Getting by can involve relentless struggle.

Conclusion

Acknowledging the capacity of people in hardship to actively shape their own lives has become a convention of stories of poverty. In welfare research this is often framed as a reaction to adversity – focusing on how people manage, manoeuvre or manipulate constraining situations. Of course, the reality of dealing with difficult circumstances and carving out a meaningful existence is inseparable in everyday life. But investment in making a *liveable* life becomes submerged in stories of bearing and bouncing back from poverty. Welfare recipients are more often positioned as adept responders than pursuers in accounts of getting by.

And yet, whether responding to the projects of powerful others or pursuing projects of one's own, shaping one's own life is not inherently positive. Recognising the different forms of agency available to people living on welfare should not assume that 'agency is good and lack of agency is bad' (Hoggett, 2001: 43). The value of ways of getting by is more varied and ambiguous than that assumption acknowledges. This point is demonstrated in research on youth friendship in strained circumstances. Carl Bonner-Thompson and Linda McDowell (2020) point to the contradictory effects of 'precarious friendships' involving drug-taking among young, white working-class men in three austerity-impacted coastal towns in England. Thayne Werdal and Lisa Mitchell (2018) also show how friendship provides acceptance, resources and protection among youth on the streets in the context of welfare retrenchment in Victoria, British Colombia. However, media and policy rhetoric often cast friendship among youth on the streets as risky and delinquent, with the result that friendships 'can serve to heighten vulnerability to surveillance and control' (Werdal and Mitchell, 2018: 320).

In-depth research provides insight into the sometimes-subtle ways that people enrich difficult lives on welfare without seeing them through rose-tinted glasses. The examples I have highlighted may seem minor or inconsequential, but they matter because they sustain a sense of purpose, satisfaction and accomplishment. More than that, mundane practices of care and upkeep (re)generate social relationships and the possibility of a meaningful life lived with others. Recognising how hope and desire endure even amid hardship requires neither centring suffering nor falling back on naive optimism.

8

Conclusion:
From problems to possibilities

Goorie[1] author Melissa Lucashenko's (2013) award-winning essay on doing it tough in the 'Black Belt' is notable not only for its searing and explicit account of life in poverty, told from the perspective of an insider. It also stands out as one of the few pieces of non-fiction in which Indigenous and minority ethnic experiences are woven seamlessly into the story of getting by on welfare. The 'Black Belt' is how Aboriginal people refer to the 'geographical-cum-cultural entity' stretching across greater Brisbane, where 'the Aboriginal underclass has historically concentrated' and live alongside poor whites in clusters of public housing. Lucashenko brings to life the quiet hope that sustains people amid grinding hardship and severe violence rooted in trauma and racism. Selma, a refugee from Yugoslavia and mother to four Aboriginal boys, is one of the three women whose story she tells. As Lucashenko describes it, when Selma spoke of her dreams for the future, 'her voice lacked certainty, and was almost wistful, in sharp contrast to when she speaks of what she has survived'. More tangible for Selma was going hungry so her boys would not, and the strength she drew from mothering them.

Anglo-settler, Indigenous and minority ethnic stories of life on welfare are not often brought together and told side by side. More often, 'ethnic' and Indigenous experiences of welfare are separated or sidelined from the 'mainstream' accounts. There is, of course, good reason to single out the specificities of Indigenous and minority ethnic experiences of welfare given the histories and structures of exclusion and intervention that have characterised efforts to deal with difference in the welfare state. However, the result can be an inadvertent whitewashing of academic accounts of lived experiences of welfare.

This book contributes to welfare research by showing how the diverse range of people I encountered shared common practical challenges and indignities despite differences of culture or ethnicity. At the same time, looking closely at the details of individual lives has also afforded insight into the more subtle shades of experience shaped by distinct ways of making sense of and relating to family, community and the nation-state. As Lisa McKenzie's (2015) research on a housing estate in the UK shows, ethnography is well positioned to make sense of the multicultural fabric of working-class cultures. On the other hand, the complexity of urban diversity and welfare system fragmentation disrupts ethnographic aims of 'immersion and wholeness' (Berg and Sigona, 2013: 347), a point I address in Appendix A.

This book also shows the importance of refashioning a welfare system that creates possibilities rather than problems for the people who rely on it. I arrive at this claim informed by the empirical insights from the study at hand, my familiarity with wider scholarship, and my knowledge as someone still embroiled in impoverished lives on welfare. There is mounting evidence across predominantly English-speaking rich countries that mean welfare exacerbates and entrenches the poverty and the vulnerability it claims to tackle (to name only a handful, see Fletcher et al, 2016; Patrick, 2017a; Smith-Carrier, 2017; Gray, 2019; Peterie et al, 2020).

This book contributes to that evidence by showing how lack of money makes life course disruptions and everyday emergencies potentially catastrophic, and lack of dignity makes it harder to rebound from them. It also shows how people find ways to make life liveable despite the problems that meagre and conditional welfare creates. However, making a liveable life on welfare does not necessarily resemble the versions of resilience that practitioners, policymakers or scholars look for among welfare users. A perspective that is sensitive to culture and context should be expected to challenge expectations of 'good resilience' and 'good outcomes' (Ungar, 2008). Moreover, hope, despite hardship, does not justify leaving people to fend for themselves; it signals the possibilities if people could focus their energy on thriving rather than simply surviving.

Welfare users and practitioners alike told me that Australia's welfare system lacked understanding. For some, 'understanding' simply meant making allowances for individual circumstances. As one caseworker put it, 'it [the income support system] could be a bit more understanding of the barriers that make it hard to meet mutual obligation requirements'. For Matilda, an experienced practitioner, understanding was associated with professional humility. 'Let them tell you their story, don't assume you know their story', she told me, although she admitted that fending off the presumptions was easier said than done.

For others, understanding required incorporating 'people who have been through it' into the welfare apparatus. Kane and Nessa wanted to see more Aboriginal workers in employment services and programmes: 'It would be more comfortable for us, like you know. [Someone who] knows where we're coming from. [Who has] got a lot of family that's probably like us.' Even Monica, who was convinced that welfare payments should be given with a firm hand, wanted to see the practical knowledge of welfare recipients incorporated into policy design. 'You can't know something if you've never seen it', she told me. Monica talked about the distance between herself and policymakers as stemming 'from a lack of education because they haven't been exposed to it'.

But respecting the insights and experience of welfare users is easier said than done. Even supportive welfare practice can involve mixed feelings about welfare users' practical knowledge of welfare systems. Practitioner judgements of welfare user knowledge and initiative are entangled with cultural ideas about vulnerability, empowerment and dependency. Even when vulnerability is deployed to push back against the harsh effects of punitive welfare, it rests on the assumed lack of knowledge and 'weaker agency' of 'the most vulnerable' (Fletcher et al, 2016: 183).

Understanding is not necessarily positive, either, when it relies on welfare users telling personal stories. Welfare systems that run on proof and disclosure can undermine dignity and hold back those unwilling or unable to tell their story convincingly or in enough detail. This is relevant to services geared toward maintaining user engagement with intensive supports – as is the growing trend in residualised social housing (Clarke et al, 2020) – as well as services preoccupied with mutual obligation metrics and compliance, such as the welfare-to-work model of employment assistance (O'Sullivan et al, 2021). Welfare systems that reserve the most support for only the very worst off make repeated disclosure a requirement. The exposure and indignity that disclosure can produce is situated not only in immediate power imbalances on the front line of welfare provision, but also in particular histories and biographies of race and inequality. The demand for disclosure may also work for or against people with different dispositions – personal or cultural – to privacy or self-narration, although this is a lingering question that requires further attention.

We've seen a glimpse of what an alternative welfare system could look like. When the pandemic hit Australia in early 2020, the federal government stepped up to support citizens, introducing the JobKeeper Payment to keep people in work, and effectively doubling the lowest income support payments by adding a $550 per fortnight 'Coronavirus Supplement'. Pension and Carer Allowance payment recipients missed out on the Supplement, instead receiving a one-off 'Economic Support Payment' of $750. But most people receiving the lowest income support payments were suddenly lifted above the poverty line, measured as the median household income of the population, and spared from mutual obligation. On a website called '550 Reasons to Smile', people used to barely scraping by on the minimum level of support shared stories of the possibilities and relief afforded by the increased payment. Most of my family members were ironically the most financially secure they had been in a long time; fear of the virus was coupled with a strange sense of relief.

The reprieve was short-lived for most and never arrived for some. Temporary Visa holders were explicitly excluded from the federal support package despite many being hit hardest by the loss of jobs in heavily casualised industries, such as hospitality and retail (Berg and Farbenblum, 2020).

Australia was one of few countries to lock them out. By September 2020, the Coronavirus Supplement had been phased down to $150 per fortnight, before stopping on 28 March 2021. A Raise the Rate campaign had seized the opportunity to push anew for a permanent increase of the minimum payments. The Australian government responded with a $50 per fortnight increase, taking JobSeeker and similar payments from the lowest to the second lowest in the Organisation for Economic Co-operation and Development (Whiteford and Bradbury, 2021). Mutual obligation requirements resumed, and an attempt to make the trial of cashless welfare payments permanent was set in motion (Klein, 2020). The Australian government began chasing people who had allegedly been overpaid $32 million in welfare money during the pandemic at the same time as it refused to make businesses pay back $180 million in wage subsidies they should not have received (Karp, 2021). The government had reverted to its begrudging approach to financial support for those most in need.

Recalling Hage's vision of the 'social gift', introduced in Chapter 3, an alternative to the current maligning spirit of welfare provision is a magnanimous one. A magnanimous welfare system would hold people up rather than kicking them when they're down. It would pay people a liveable income and entrust them to make it work for the obligations that are meaningful to them. A more generous welfare system would not magically evaporate the social problems borne out of already entrenched poverty and inequality. And it would only be the starting point for transforming 'attitudes, environments and practices that disable, discriminate and disadvantage' (Redmond et al, 2022: 8). But it would mean that a hostile welfare system is not one of the problems wearing people down and making a life they value, however it is imagined, further out of reach. A generous spirit of welfare would honour shared humanity rather than approaching those who are worse off with either contempt or pity. It would work for rather than against a liveable life.

APPENDIX A

Details about the scholarship

Addressing culture

This book sets out to account for cultural diversity in lived experiences of welfare without relying on what Michèle Lamont and Mario Luis Small (2008: 76) describe as 'thin understandings of culture'. They argue that poverty and inequality studies have tended to see culture as 'a group's norms and values, as its attitudes towards work and family, or as patterns of behaviour' (Lamont and Small, 2008: 76). This can imply that culture is something that is fixed and pre-existing. In contrast, cultural sociology, anthropology and cultural studies have developed ideas of culture as a *process* of making and remaking shared understandings, customs and codes of behaviour in practice. Cultural formations are more likely to be understood as provisional and porous according to these approaches than fixed or unified. Rather than 'imputing a shared culture to groups', the emphasis is on 'how individuals make sense of their lives' (Lamont and Small, 2008: 79) and 'the conditions under which people's stories of themselves are constructed' (Couldry, 2000: 52).

Approaching culture with care is critical given that both welfare policy and multiculturalism have oversimplified and reified class and ethnic group identity and difference (Berg and Sigona, 2013). I aimed to address ethnicity head on, but without assuming it was the most important factor conditioning and differentiating experiences of welfare. This required an approach that is 'sensitive to ethnicity in the empirical world, but does not impose it where it is not' (Fox and Jones, 2013: 394). Importantly, this approach does not assume that ethnicity and culture are synonymous.

Cultural explanations of poverty have driven criticism of the corrupting influence of 'passive' welfare and the rise of conditional support as a corrective to welfare dependency. The idea that poor people live according to a distinct subculture of dysfunctional values and behaviours that perpetuate poverty is well worn but resilient. So is the racist portrayal of poor Black communities as most afflicted by such cultural dysfunction. As I outline in Chapter 2, these ideas have been hugely influential in Australia and elsewhere in making social security and other forms of social support targeted at the most marginal members of society more directive and supervisory. Using welfare measures to change the behaviour of welfare recipients and bring it in line with mainstream values is by now a well-established orthodoxy.

Even in attempts to make social services more responsive to minority groups, thin understandings of culture can inadvertently cast people marked as 'culturally different' as the problem. Recognition of distinct needs can give rise to a 'problem-centred approach' that characterises ethnic groups as having their own specific problems that need to be addressed (Chalmers and Allon, 2002: 3). Besides casting ethnic groups as overly coherent, this approach neglects the cultural underpinnings of welfare agencies and government processes, which are neither straightforward nor uniform. As anthropologist Emma Kowal (2008: 340) observes in relation to Indigenous health policy, it is made up of 'many over-lapping subcultures [including] policy, bureaucratic, activist, and professional'.

I take 'responsibility' and 'vulnerability' as starting points to explore how dominant cultural scripts about need and support interact with the diverse versions of obligation that make up everyday life. The idea of cultural scripts refers to the institutions – understood loosely as the taken-for-granted expectations, rules, routines and schemas – that orient shared ways of thinking, feeling and acting (Lamont and Small, 2008: 89). Paying attention to cultural scripts 'requires paying attention less on individuals and more on structures and institutions, including the cultural and social mechanisms that maintain classification systems' (Lamont and Small, 2008: 90). This approach foregrounds the contextual and contested politics of needs interpretation (Fraser, 1989), drawing attention to the conditions under which certain definitions are given prominence and authorised in public discourse.

Responsibility and vulnerability are also fertile analytic concepts that strike at the core of the human condition as social beings. This makes them useful frames for thinking through the interface between culturally diverse ways of life and welfare institutions. Responsibility is integral to social identity and belonging. As Ghassan Hage (2012: 112) puts it: 'Claims of responsibility are claims about the degree and the nature of one's social and emotional enmeshment in the collectivity one feels responsible to.' Vulnerability is also 'fundamentally social and relational' in character; as interdependent beings humans are susceptible to the actions of others and forces beyond their control (Mackenzie et al, 2014: 6). 'Responsibility' and 'vulnerability' take on lived complexity as the book shows how a diverse group of welfare users relate to contemporary regimes of social support based on ideas of mutual obligation and partnership.

This book foregrounds the lived experience of a mix of people navigating this welfare landscape. Claire Alexander and colleagues (2012: 4) identify the payoffs and risks of foregrounding cultural diversity. They acknowledge the important contribution of using cultural diversity as it is lived in the everyday 'to render the lives and experiences of people, communities and minorities visible in all their richness, complexity and humanity'. But, they warn, 'such rich tapestries need to also examine, and place themselves within, a broader set of economic, political and social contexts and transformations – to (re)place culture and identity as a site of struggle, constraint and resistance'. With this warning in mind, I endeavour to keep in view both the messiness of everyday lived existence and the wider conditions in which it is placed.

A place-based study

This book is based on my PhD in Sociology. I spent 18 months between January 2014 and June 2015 conducting ethnographic fieldwork in southwest Sydney. My research was broadly contained in the Bankstown Local Government Area, which was amalgamated with the eastern neighbouring Canterbury Council in 2016 after I had finished my fieldwork. The most recent available census figures from 2016 for southwest Sydney therefore include suburbs stretching right up to the inner western suburbs of Sydney. My research was based in what are now three of the five wards that make up the amalgamated City of Canterbury Bankstown: the central Bankstown Ward, and the Bass Hill Ward and Revesby Ward to the west.

Southwest Sydney has a long history of Indigenous occupation that predates invasion by tens of thousands of years. The Bankstown area was a transitional region originally occupied by the Dharawal and Darug peoples (Rosen, 1996: 9). The area was one of the first frontiers of European occupation, and the original Aboriginal population was decimated by violence and disease (Yamanouchi, 2010: 219). However, as George Morgan (2006: 1– 10) describes, Aboriginal people maintained a presence in Sydney, building camps in and around European settlements. From the 1960s the establishment of the government housing programme, Housing for Aborigines (HFA), created a massive increase in the number of Aboriginal people living in suburban areas (Morgan, 2006: 62). Today, the majority of the Indigenous metropolitan population lives dispersed in suburban housing, and 'there is no single unified Aboriginal community in western Sydney' but 'there are groupings, nodes and networks as well as isolated Koori families' (Cowlishaw, 2011: 179). Only 0.7 per cent of residents in Canterbury-Bankstown City identified as Indigenous in the 2016 census, a smaller proportion than the neighbouring Blacktown (2.8 per cent) and Campbelltown City (3.8 per cent) areas and Greater Sydney (1.5 per cent) (.id consulting, nd-a, nd-b).

Southwest Sydney has figured in the popular imagination as the heartland of cultural diversity since the post-Second World War immigration programme to provide lower skilled, low-paid labour transformed the region with large-scale resettlement of immigrants from non-English-speaking backgrounds (Collins et al, 2000: 106). Southwest Sydney is often described as one of the most multicultural areas in Australia. Sixty per cent of people in the Bankstown-Canterbury area spoke a language other than English at home in 2016. Zooming in on the Bankstown Ward at the centre of the City area, this figure jumps to 72 per cent. Forty-four per cent of Canterbury-Bankstown residents were born overseas, compared to 36 per cent in Greater Sydney (for all the statistics that follow, see .id consulting, nd–c).

The Canterbury Bankstown area is known for being a centre of Lebanese and Vietnamese settlement since the 1980s. Lebanese was the largest self-identified ancestry group in Canterbury Bankstown in 2016, at 15 per cent, but was even higher in the areas where my research was based: 26 per cent in the Bankstown Ward and 22 per cent in the Bass Hill Ward. Vietnamese was in the top two ancestries nominated in the Bankstown Ward (11.5 per cent) and the top three in the Bass Hill Ward (12.8 per cent), after Australian (14.8 per cent). Lebanese and Vietnamese were less prominent in the Revesby Ward, where the top ancestry responses were Australian (25 per cent), English (22.5 per cent) and Chinese (10 per cent). Across the Canterbury-Bankstown City, including the three wards where I focused my research, the number of Lebanese, Vietnamese and Chinese residents increased between 2011 and 2016. Pakistani was a notable emerging group in the Bankstown Ward, with 882 more people nominating Pakistani ancestry than the previous census.

More Canterbury-Bankstown residents worked in healthcare and social assistance than any other area in 2016 (10.8 per cent), an increase of 4,867 in a decade. Employment in the region is still concentrated in industries vulnerable to economic downturn, such as Manufacturing (6.6 per cent), Transport, Postal and Warehousing (7.7 per cent), Construction (9.5 per cent) and Retail Trade (10.4 per cent). There were 4,957 fewer people employed in manufacturing in 2016 than measured a decade prior. The decline of manufacturing in southwestern Sydney has left the Muslim-Lebanese population in particular exposed to unemployment as they were more likely to be employed as unskilled workers compared to Christian-Lebanese small business owners (Collins et al, 2000: 106).

While there are varying levels of disadavtange across Canterbury-Bankstown, overall the City scores low on the SEIFA Index of Disadvantage, an area-based index that ranks relative socio-economic disadvantage using indicators such as low income, low educational attainment and high unemployment and unskilled employment. A lower score indicates more disadvantage. The Bankstown Ward is in the 9th percentile, meaning 91 per cent of areas are better off. The Bass Hill Ward is in the 10th percentile, while the Revesby Ward is in the 49th percentile.

In 2012, as I was formulating the research project, the former Bankstown City became one of five designated 'disadvantaged areas' targeted for the trial of place-based income management. The measure involved the compulsory quarantining of a percentage of welfare payments onto a card that could only be used to buy approved items at approved stores. According to the Department of Social Services (cited by Buckmaster, 2012) it was 'chosen based on a number of factors including unemployment levels, youth unemployment, skills gaps, the numbers of people receiving welfare payments, and the length of time people have been on income support payments'. Alongside the controversial measure, the local community sector had an influx of federal funding from the Communities for Children initiative, aimed at bolstering early intervention and family services. It was also targeted under the Teenage Parent and Jobless Family Measures from 2012 that required teenage parents receiving welfare payments and parents without income for more than two years to fulfil additional participation requirements such as interviews with Centrelink and training – converted into ParentsNext projects in 2016 (Australian Government, 2019).

A fine-grained qualitative approach

My fieldwork included in-depth interviews with 25 residents and 11 interviews with frontline community welfare staff, as well as participant observation in community welfare organisations and more limited time spent with a small number of families. I spent more time with some of the people I interviewed, conducting follow-up interviews with a few, seeing some regularly at family support programmes run by local community organisations or at local community events, and accompanying a handful as they ran errands or invited me to their homes. Prolonged involvement in a setting lends itself to a closer understanding of the ways of seeing and doing things that make up everyday life and the exploration of culture as a process rather than an object (Denzin and Lincoln, 2008: 14).

The relational work that an ethnographic approach involves takes time and commitment. I spent three months volunteering and 'hanging around' before I approached anyone for an interview. This allowed me to become a familiar face while also lending my skills and time to the local communities I sought to engage. I volunteered and observed at a small and eclectic organisation housing a range of programmes with different funding channels, including child and family support programmes and ethno-specific community groups. The volunteer observation involved an intensive period of six months working two to four days a week in various roles, including menial tasks such as filing and auditing assets, lending my research skills to a policy audit and helping set up and run playgroups and other family support activities. This gave me first-hand experience of various family support programmes, and access to some of its internal documents and administrative processes. Volunteering in the organisation facilitated contact with an interagency network of frontline workers and opened opportunities to participate in other activities and programmes, including two days observing Emergency Relief when the opportunity arose.

Participating in family support programmes and regularly attending community events also introduced me to potential interviewees who then referred me on to others. Interviews with welfare users elicited information about networks and practices of support, experiences of social security and support services, roles and duties in the family, civic, national and transnational spheres and views about the government's role in providing support. I spoke to people primarily of working age between 20 and 64, except for three pensioners. The majority of people I interviewed were parents of younger children. I interviewed 5 single parents and 13 partnered with children. Most of them received either Parenting Payment (single), Parenting Payment (partnered) or Newstart Allowance (unemployment payments) depending on the age of their children and their partnered status. Two were ineligible for income support as a newly arrived migrant and asylum seeker. I also interviewed two young men with no dependants, one on Youth Allowance and the other unemployed but refusing benefits, and one woman surviving on the Disability Support Pension (see Appendix B for information about key payments).

I interviewed 7 men and 18 women of Lebanese, Pakistani, Chinese, Aboriginal and Anglo backgrounds. These groups were purposively selected to include more established and emergent migrant populations in the southwest Sydney area and varying lengths of residency in Australia. The mix of groups also aimed to reflect the character of diversity arising from Australia's settler-colonial and immigration history. The Lebanese-Australian interview participants were all Muslim and second-generation migrants, while the Pakistani interviewees were also Muslim, but newly or recently arrived residents in Australia. All of the Chinese participants were born in China (or Hong Kong), but had lived in Australia for between 10 and 30 years. I only interviewed people who spoke proficient English, but I made information sheets available in Arabic, Mandarin and Urdu to ensure informed consent.

I sought out people from selected countries instead of the broader category of people from culturally and linguistically diverse backgrounds to allow for different welfare cultures and family models as a common point of reference. However, these ethnic and national categories were approached 'reflexively' by not assuming group commonalities or the salience of shared ethnicity or nationality (Amelina and Faist, 2012: 1711). The choice to target across a range of groups reflected early aspirations for a comparative analysis, but challenges recruiting and the pressures of time-limited PhD candidature meant I was unable to follow through. The spread of people I spoke to from each of the categories was varied and uneven, and the numbers too small to make comparisons across ethnic or national groupings. The small number of people engaged in the research is a trade-off for the nuance and depth that an intensive and relational approach offers. A culturally sensitive analysis is still possible without assigning common traits to groups.

I also interviewed frontline workers engaged in family support and community development from a handful of non-profit community welfare organisations, employed as either therapists, case managers, youth workers or community development officers. Respondents tended to be either qualified in the human services professions of social work or therapies, or had general qualifications such as a social science degree. Their experience in social services ranged from a few months to a couple of decades. Most were women, except for two men, reflecting the strong predominance of women in the community services sector (Meagher and Healy, 2005). Their cultural and linguistic diversity mirrored the area in which they worked, contrary to the profile of the wider sector, which is less culturally diverse than both the Australian community and the broader workforce (Meagher and Healy, 2005).

Intimacy is both a strength and a dilemma of prolonged and close engagement with people for research. In-depth and open-ended methods can be more 'attuned' to the voices and perspectives of people involved in the research, allowing them to explain their feelings and experiences in their own words (Liamputtong, 2007: 7–9). This is important in research about people that often figure as the objects of welfare rhetoric even as their own voices are sidelined. But intimacy may also lead to over-disclosure and leave people feeling exposed when their life is laid bare, not least when welfare users are keenly aware that they are culturally disparaged as burdensome and failed citizens (Sinding and Aronson, 2003: 109). Likewise, volunteering as a form of participant observation 'provides space to form relationships that are not solely focused on the researchers' needs and objectives' (Garthwaite, 2016: 63). But it also involves an ongoing negotiation of boundaries as the volunteer observer's research goals potentially blur with their roles as helper, colleague, ally or confidant. As a researcher in training, I found that some people wanted to help me with my PhD project, perhaps seeing me as student rather than as a researcher proper. The negotiation of boundaries continued during analysis with the need to maintain a critical and reflexive lens despite my feelings of attachment to the people I had spent time with.

Intimacy therefore calls for the ongoing negotiation of consent. During participant observation, I introduced myself to all staff, service users and partner agencies as a researcher and, if I had recurring contact with them, reminded them of my research goals as time passed. I asked for verbal consent at the outset of interviews and 'go-alongs' with welfare users, but also confirmed consent as the research unfolded. I tried to be sensitive to cues of tone and silence that told me topics were off-limits, as well as approaching sensitive or probing questions 'tentatively' and providing 'ready exits' to respondents (Sinding and Aronson, 2003: 109). I reached out to individuals whose story features prominently in this book to ensure they were still comfortable sharing it in publication given that time and their lives have moved on since they opened up to me. This wasn't always possible as the contact details I had for some were not current and I was unsuccessful in tracking them down.

Ethnography is challenging in a diverse suburban context and a fragmented welfare landscape. Urban diversity and welfare system fragmentation 'challenge[s] ethnographic ideals of "immersion and wholeness"' (Berg and Sigona, 2013: 347). I was not embedded in a single local community despite the study being geographically contained. My efforts to engage ethno-specific organisations and government agencies were less successful, contributing to a somewhat piecemeal view of an anyway dispersed welfare landscape. Ethnography also comes up against the ethical and practical limits of observing the everyday routines of family life. Christina articulated this best. After our first interview she had agreed to let me join her for a day while she ran errands, but later changed her mind after her grandmother said it was inappropriate to have someone 'follow you around all day'. As a result, my analysis relies more heavily on formal interviews than some ethnographers would favour. In-depth, semi-structured interviews provided glimpses into the more intimate spheres of everyday experience and how they were narrated, albeit after the fact and inevitably told with the researcher as audience in mind. I approached interviews ethnographically as an immersive encounter (Hockey and Forsey, 2012), writing field notes about the scene and other non-verbal aspects of the interview. Participant observation added context and depth to my interpretation of the interview data.

An ethnographic sensibility shaped my analysis of interview transcripts and observation notes. I manually coded to identify larger themes in the details of the data, beginning primarily with data-driven codes. These codes were refined and became more conceptual with each sweep of the data. Coding allowed me to break apart and piece together the data to get a sense of patterns and themes related to the topics I was interested in (Saldaña, 2009). However, I also wrote portraits of participants that were more attuned to sequence, complexity and contradiction in their accounts. I listened to the audio recordings of interviews a number of times to ensure the 'live' dimensions of the interviews were not abstracted out of excerpts and that quotes were not decontextualised from the interview as a whole. These techniques promoted a contextual and holistic interpretation of the data, limiting the isolation and cherry-picking of quotes as evidence.

A small-scale, qualitative study does not aspire to make claims that are representative of the broader population. But it does aspire to say something of relevance and reach beyond the confines of the particular site and participants included in the study. While the insights presented in this book are grounded in individual and highly situated stories, the rich detail and the conceptual arguments the book offers give it 'resonance', to borrow Sarah Tracy's (2010: 844) phrasing, beyond the empirical particulars.

Recruitment procedure and ethics

The Macquarie University Human Research Ethics Committee approved the project.

The research for the project was largely conducted through local community organisations. After initial meetings with the executive officers of participating organisations, I emailed them the aims and boundaries of the research and asked them to confirm their agreement in writing. All staff at the organisations was made aware that I was a researcher, as were the clients and agency partners I encountered while volunteering.

Both of the organisations I volunteered with had strong and longstanding relationships with local Aboriginal Elders and residents. This was particularly valuable in enabling me to get to know some leaders and members of local Aboriginal communities. All Aboriginal interviewees were recruited through Aboriginal-specific programmes run by these organisations, and Aboriginality was defined by self and community identification. Ethnicity was defined broadly in terms of common national ancestry and language reflected in the targeting of Pakistani, Chinese and Lebanese participants (although care was taken to be attentive to differentiation within these categories).

I recruited welfare users for interviews primarily with the help of community welfare organisations. I would explain to potential participants that I was interested in hearing their stories of being on welfare, what they thought of the welfare system and what kind of support they wanted and needed. I suggested I follow up by contacting them with more information, giving potential participants a chance to think about a subsequent meeting and avoid coercion.

Potential participants were provided with an information letter explaining the study and the interview process. While interviews were confined to people proficient in English, information sheets were made available in the native languages of target groups to ensure informed consent. A verbal lay account of the content of the information sheet was also given, emphasising that participation was voluntary and participants could withdraw at any time. Given the potential mistrust of authority among some people of migrant background, Indigenous people and marginal welfare recipients, I sought verbal consent to mitigate participants feeling uncomfortable with signing a written consent form. I gave interview participants a $20 Coles Myer Gift Card after each interview to thank them for contributing their time and stories to the study. These aspects of recruitment, engagement and reimbursement accord with the Australian Institute of Aboriginal and Torres Strait Islander Studies protocols for conducting research with Aboriginal people (AIATSIS, 2012).

Some people who had already been interviewed and with whom I had developed a rapport were invited to participate further by having me join them while they carried out aspects of their routines, such as running errands or attending community activities. In the few cases where this took place, a new information sheet setting out the aims and boundaries of the observation was offered and verbally explained, and verbal consent sought for each visit.

Frontline community welfare workers were emailed an invitation to participate in 30-minute interviews via their staff email address with the permission and assistance of organisation managers.

I also encountered staff while volunteering at a community welfare organisation over a period of 18 months and at interagency events associated with that volunteer work. As with welfare users, I would explain the study and offer to follow up by contacting them with more information or to confirm their interest in participating to avoid coercion.

I also conducted participant observation of selected projects and sessions during my time as a volunteer, looking out for how service users and staff defined need, client and staff expectations of support, and the agency's relationship with other institutions. The supervising staff members were informed of the boundaries of the observation, and clients and agency partners in attendance were made aware that I was a researcher and told they could choose to be omitted from field notes. Relevant observations were recorded in a notebook after each session, in which neither staff nor clients were identified.

Steps were taken to de-identify participants in the write-up of the findings. All names are fictionalised and some quotes are not attributed to specific participants. The work roles and cultural backgrounds of staff have been detached from quotes to protect their anonymity. In some cases participants have been de-gendered or minor details changed.

Key Australian benefits and pensions

Payment type	Maximum rate* per fortnight 2015**	Maximum rate* per fortnight 2022**	Basic eligibility
Youth Allowance (YA) (single, no dependants)	AU$426.80 (away from home) AU$281.00 (at home 18+)	AU$530.40 (away from home) AU$367.00 (at home 18+)	• Means- and asset-tested • Looking for full-time work or doing approved activities • Mutual obligation requirements for jobseekers • 18–21 for jobseekers • 18–24 if studying full time or doing a full-time Australian Apprenticeship • Australian resident 2+ years (2015) or 4+ years (2022)
Unemployment benefit (single, no dependants)	AU$519.2 (NSA)	AU$642.70 (JSP)	• Means- and asset-tested • Unemployed • 22+
Formerly Newstart Allowance (NSA) Replaced by JobSeeker Payment (JSP)			• Mutual obligation requirements • Australian resident 2+ years (2015) or 4+ years (2022)
Parenting Payment (PP) (single) (includes Pension Supplement)	AU$725.40	AU$880.20	• Means- and asset-tested • Principle carer for child under eight years • Australian resident 2+ years (2015) or 4+ years (2022) • Mutual obligation requirements when youngest child turns six or if a compulsory ParentsNext participant***
Parenting Payment (PP) (partnered)	AU$468.80	AU$585.30	• Means- and asset-tested • Youngest child aged under six • Australian resident 2+ years (2015) or 4+ years (2022) • Mutual obligation requirements for compulsory ParentsNext recipients***

Payment type	Maximum rate* per fortnight 2015**	Maximum rate* per fortnight 2022**	Basic eligibility
Disability Support Pension (DSP) (includes Pension Supplement)	AU$846.10 (single) AU$637.80 (partnered)	AU$973.50 (single) AU$733.8 (partnered)	• Means- and asset-tested • 21+ • Unable to work 15 hours • Impairment rating of 20 points or more • Australian resident 10+years
Age Pension (includes Pension Supplement)	AU$846.10 (single) AU$637.80 (partnered)	AU$973.50 (single) AU$733.8 (partnered)	• Means- and asset-tested • Age 65–67 and over (depending on birth date) • Australian resident 10+ years

Note: * Does not include supplementary assistance, such as the Energy Supplement or Rent Assistance. Pension Supplement included where eligible. The Pension Supplement was introduced as part of Goods and Services Tax (GST) reforms in 2000 to ensure pensioners were not disadvantaged by price increases.

** All rates as of 20 March, except pensions.

*** ParentsNext is an intensive intervention programme targeted at parents with children under six. It was trialled in 10 local government areas from 1 April 2016, and then launched nationally from 1 July 2018.

Sources: https://guides.dss.gov.au/social-security-guide/5/2/1/50;

https://guides.dss.gov.au/social-security-guide/5/2/1/20;

https://guides.dss.gov.au/social-security-guide/5/2/4/50;

https://guides.dss.gov.au/social-security-guide/5/2/2/10;

https://guides.dss.gov.au/social-security-guide/5/2/8/10

Notes

Chapter 1

[1] The Indigenous population in Australia includes Aboriginal people and Torres Strait Islanders. While 'Aboriginal people' is often used to refer to Indigenous people of mainland Australia, these are colonisers' terms that fail to capture the distinct and diverse range of Indigenous cultures and nations belonging to specific lands. In this book I follow the participants' lead and refer to them as 'Aboriginal'. In the context of family and community life and welfare in southwest Sydney, being 'Black' was often expressed as more salient than specific relations to Country. The legacy of government child removal policies meant that kin and/or Country relatedness was severed for some people, but some found alternative terms of participation in local Aboriginal culture and community (Yamanouchi, 2010).

Chapter 2

[1] The Guugu Yimithirr people are from far north Queensland.

Chapter 5

[1] Under the PBS the Commonwealth government subsidises the cost of medicine. It also offers subsidies for specialist consultations through Medicare, but only 30 per cent of appointments are bulk-billed, and unregulated prices mean patients can be left substantially out of pocket (see Sivey, 2016).

Chapter 6

[1] TAFE stands for 'technical and further education'. These institutes deliver and assess nationally recognised vocational training (VET), and issue nationally recognised qualifications.

Chapter 7

[1] Unangax̂ refers to the first people of the Aleutian Islands region of southwestern Alaska.

Chapter 8

[1] Goorie refers to Aboriginal people from the north coast of New South Wales. Lucashenko identifies as Bundjalung and European.

References

.id consulting (nd-a) Blacktown City Council community profile. Available at: https://profile.id.com.au/blacktown/highlights-2016

.id consulting (nd-b) Campbelltown City Council community profile. Available at: https://profile.id.com.au/campbelltown/highlights-2016

.id consulting (nd-c) City of Canterbury Bankstown community profile. Available at: https://profile.id.com.au/canterbury-bankstown

Abdel-Fattah, R. (2016) '"Lebanese Muslim": a Bourdieuian "capital" offense in an Australian coastal town', *Journal of Intercultural Studies*, 37: 323–38.

Alexander, C., Kaur, R. and St Louis, B. (2012) 'Identities: new directions in uncertain times', *Identities*, 19: 1–7.

Altman, J.C. (2011) 'A genealogy of "demand sharing": from the pure anthropology to public policy', in Y. Musharbash and M. Barber (eds) *Ethnography and the Production of Anthropological Knowledge: Essays in Honour of Nicolas Peterson*, Canberra: ANU E Press, pp 187–200.

Altman, J.C. and Sanders, W. (1991) *From Exclusion to Dependence: Aborigines and the Welfare State in Australia*, Canberra: Centre for Aboriginal Economic Policy Research (CAEPR).

Amelina, A. and Faist, T. (2012) 'De-naturalizing the national in research methodologies: key concepts of transnational studies in migration', *Ethnic and Racial Studies*, 35(10): 1707–1724

Amin, A. (2010) 'The remainders of race', *Theory, Culture & Society*, 27: 1–23.

Anderson, J. and Honneth, A. (2005) 'Autonomy, vulnerability, recognition and justice', in J. Christman and J. Anderson (eds) *Autonomy and the Challenges of Liberalism: New Essays*, Cambridge: Cambridge University Press, pp 127–49.

Andres, L. and Round, J. (2015) 'The role of "persistent resilience" within everyday life and polity: households coping with marginality within the "Big Society"', *Environment and Planning A*, 47: 676–90.

Appadurai, A. (2004) 'The capacity to aspire: culture and the terms of recognition', *Culture and Public Action*, 59–84.

Atkin, K. and Chattoo, S. (2007) 'The dilemmas of providing welfare in an ethnically diverse state: seeking reconciliation in the role of a "reflexive practitioner"', *Policy & Politics*, 35(3): 377–93.

Atkinson, D.C. (2017) *The Burden of White Supremacy: Containing Asian Migration in the British Empire and the United States*, Chapel Hill: The University of Northern Carolina Press.

Atwood, B. and Markus, A. (1999) 'Introduction', in B. Attwood and A. Markus (eds) *The Struggle for Aboriginal Rights: A Documentary History*, Crows Nest, NSW: Allen & Unwin, pp 1–29.

Australian Government (2018) 'Multicultural Australia: united, strong, successful', Canberra. Available from: www.homeaffairs.gov.au/mca/Statements/english-multicultural-statement.pdf

Australian Government (2019) '1.1.P.57 ParentsNext'. Available from: http://guides.dss.gov.au/guide-social-security-law/1/1/p/57

Australian Institute of Family (2015) *History of Child Protection Services*, Australian Government.

Australian Institute of Health and Welfare (2017) *Child Protection Australia 2015–2016*, Child Welfare Series No 66, Canberra, ACT.

Back, L. (2015) 'Why everyday life matters: class, community and making life livable', *Sociology*, 49: 820–36.

Berg, L. and Farbenblum B. (2020) *As if We Weren't Humans: The Abandonment of Temporary Migrants in Australia during COVID-19*. Migrant Worker Justice Initiative.

Berg, M.L. and Sigona, N. (2013) 'Ethnography, diversity and urban space', *Identities*, 20: 347–60.

Best, J. (2013) 'Redefining poverty as risk and vulnerability: shifting strategies of liberal economic governance', *Third World Quarterly*, 34: 109–29.

Bielefeld, S. (2018) 'Cashless welfare transfers for "vulnerable" welfare recipients: law, ethics and vulnerability', *Feminist Legal Studies*, 26: 1–23.

Bonner-Thompson, C. and McDowell, L. (2020) 'Precarious lives, precarious care: young men's caring practices in three coastal towns in England', *Emotion, Space and Society*, 35: 1–7. Available from: https://doi.org/10.1016/j.emospa.2020.100684

Boucher, A. (2014) 'Familialism and migrant welfare policy: restrictions on social security provision for newly arrived immigrants', *Policy & Politics*, 42: 367–84.

Brough, M., Bond, C. and Hunt, J. (2004) 'Strong in the city: towards a strength-based approach in Indigenous health promotion', *Health Promotion Journal of Australia*, 15: 215–20.

Brown, K. (2011) '"Vulnerability": handle with care', *Ethics and Social Welfare*, 5: 313–21.

Brown, K. (2014) 'Questioning the vulnerability zeitgeist: care and control practices with "vulnerable" young people', *Social Policy and Society*, 13: 371–87.

Brown, K., Ecclestone, K. and Emmel, N. (2017) 'The many faces of vulnerability', *Social Policy and Society*, 16: 497–510.

Buckmaster, L. (2012) 'New place based income management to commence 1 July', *FlagPost*, Canberra: Parliamentary Library. Available from: https://www.aph.gov.au/About_Parliament/Parliamentary_Departments/Parliamentary_Library/FlagPost/2012/June/New_Place_Based_Income_Management_to_commence_1_July

Butterworth, P. (2008) 'The experience of welfare receipt: depression, demoralisation and despair?', *Impact*, (Summer): 15–20. Available from: https://search.informit.org/doi/10.3316/ielapa.118741646851539

Cardona, B., Chalmers, S. and Neilson, B. (2006) *Diverse Strategies for Diverse Carers: The Cultural Context of Family Carers in NSW*, Centre for Cultural Research, University of Western Sydney.

Carrigan, C. (2021) 'To improve pandemic control, listen to the community leaders of western and south west Sydney', *Croaky Health Media*. Available from: https://www.croakey.org/to-improve-pandemic-control-listen-to-the-leaders-of-western-and-south-west-sydney/

Castles, F.G. (1996) 'Needs-based strategies of social protection in Australia and New Zealand', in G. Esping-Andersen (ed) *Welfare States in Transition*, London: SAGE, pp 88–115.

Caswell, D., Marston, G. and Larsen, J.E. (2010) 'Unemployed citizen or "at risk" client? Classification systems and employment services in Denmark and Australia', *Critical Social Policy*, 30: 384–404.

Chalmers, S. and Allon, F. (2002) *'We All Come from Somewhere': Cultural Diversity at Sydney Children's Hospital*, Sydney: Multicultural Health Unit, South East Sydney Area Health Service.

Chase, E. and Walker, R. (2013) 'The co-construction of shame in the context of poverty: beyond a threat to the social bond', *Sociology*, 47: 739–54.

Clarke, A., Cheshire, L. and Parsell, C. (2020) 'Bureaucratic encounters "after neoliberalism": examining the supportive turn in social housing governance', *British Journal of Sociology*, 71: 253–68.

Clarke, J. (2004) *Changing Welfare, Changing States: New Directions in Social Policy*, London: SAGE.

Collins, J., Noble, G., Poynting, S., and Tabar, P. (2000) 'The context of "ethnic crime" in Sydney: socioeconomic, cultural and spatial', in *Kebabs, Kids, Cops and Crime: Youth, Ethnicity and Crime*, Annandale: Puto Press, pp 94–135.

Considine, M. (2001) *Enterprising States: The Public Management of Welfare-to-Work*, Cambridge: Cambridge University Press.

Cortis, N. (2012) 'Overlooked and under-served? Promoting service use and engagement among "hard-to-reach" populations', *International Journal of Social Welfare*, 21: 351–60.

Cortis, N., Katz, I. and Patulny, R. (2009) *Engaging Hard-to-Reach Families and Children*, Occasional Paper No 26, Canberra, ACT.

Couldry, N. (2000) *Inside Culture*, London: SAGE.

Cowlishaw, G. (2011) 'Mythologising culture: part 2: disturbing aboriginality in the suburbs', *The Australian Journal of Anthropology*, 22: 170–88.

Curthoys, A. (2000) 'Gender studies in Australia: a history', *Australian Feminist Studies*, 15: 19–38.

Curtis, K. (2019) 'Welfare is a "hand up, not out" says Coalition', *Financial Review*, 31 July.

Davidson, P., Bradbury, B. and Dorsch, P. (2021) *Covid Income Support: Analysis of Income Support in the Covid Lockdowns in 2020 and 2021*, ACOSS/UNSW Sydney Poverty and Inequality Partnership, Build Back Fairer Series, Report no 1, Sydney.

Davis, L.V. and Hagen, J.L. (1996) 'Stereotypes and stigma: what's changed for welfare mothers', *Affilia*, 11: 319–37.

Dean, H. (2013) 'The translation of needs into rights: reconceptualising social citizenship as a global phenomenon', *International Journal of Social Welfare*, 22: S32–S49.

Denzin, N.K. and Lincoln, Y.S. (2008) 'Introduction: the discipline and practice of qualitative research', in N.K. Denzin and Y.S. Lincoln (eds) *The Landscape of Qualitative Research* (3rd edn), New York: SAGE, pp 1–43.

DeVerteuil, G. (2015) *Resilience in the Post-Welfare Inner City: Voluntary Sector Geographies in London, Los Angeles and Sydney – University of Sydney*, Bristol: Policy Press.

Dinu, L. and Scullion, L. (2019) 'Exploring the impact of welfare conditionality on Roma migrants in the UK', in P. Dwyer (ed) *Dealing with Welfare Conditionality: Implementation and Effects*, Bristol: Policy Press, pp 119–48.

Department of Social Services (2015) *Emergency Relief*, Australian Government.

Donoghue, M. and Edmiston, D. (2020) 'Gritty citizens? Exploring the logic and limits of resilience in UK social policy during times of socio-material insecurity', *Critical Social Policy*, 40: 7–29.

Dunn, C.D. (2017) 'Personal narratives and self-transformation in postindustrial societies', *Annual Review of Anthropology*, 46: 65–80.

Dwyer, P. (2000) *Welfare Rights and Responsibilities: Contesting Social Citizenship*, Bristol: Policy Press.

Dwyer, P. (2004) 'Creeping conditionality in the UK: from welfare rights to conditional entitlements?', *The Canadian Journal of Sociology*, 29: 265–87.

Dwyer, P. (2019) 'Editor's introduction', in P. Dwyer (ed) *Dealing with Welfare Conditionality: Implementation and effects*, Bristol: Policy Press, pp 1–13.

Dwyer, P. and Brown, D. (2005) 'Meeting basic needs? Forced migrants and welfare', *Social Policy and Society*, 4: 369–80.

Dwyer, P. and Wright, S. (2014) 'Universal Credit, ubiquitous conditionality and its implications for social citizenship', *Journal of Poverty and Social Justice*, 22: 27–35.

Edmiston, D. (2018) *Welfare, Inequality and Social Citizenship: Deprivation and Affluence in Austerity Britain*, Bristol: Policy Press.

Ellis, K. (2011) '"Street-level bureaucracy" revisited: the changing face of frontline discretion in adult social care in England', *Social Policy & Administration*, 45: 221–44.

Emirbayer, M. and Mische, A. (1998) 'What is agency?', *American Journal of Sociology*, 103: 962–1023.

Emmel, N. and Hughes, K. (2010) '"Recession, it's all the same to us son": the longitudinal experience (1999–2010) of deprivation', *Twenty-First Century Society*, 5: 171–81.

Evans, T. (2011) 'Professionals, managers and discretion: critiquing street-level bureaucracy', *British Journal of Social Work*, 41: 368–86.

Fineman, M.A. (2016) 'Equality, autonomy, and the vulnerable subject in law and politics', in M.A. Fineman and A. Grear (eds) *Vulnerability: Reflections on a New Ethical Foundation for Law and Politics*, Abingdon: Routledge, pp 13–27.

Fletcher, D.R., Flint, J., Batty, E. and McNeill, J. (2016) 'Gamers or victims of the system? Welfare reform, cynical manipulation and vulnerability', *Journal of Poverty and Social Justice*, 24: 171–85.

Flint, J. (2009) 'Subversive subjects and conditional, earned and denied citizenship', in M. Barnes and D. Prior (eds) *Subversive Citizenship: Power, Agency and Resistance in Public Services*, Bristol: Policy Press, pp 83–98.

Fook, J. (2012) *Social Work: A Critical Approach to Practice*, Los Angeles, London, New Delhi and Singapore: SAGE.

Fowkes, L. (2019) *The Application of Income Support Obligations and Penalties in to Remote Indigenous Australians, 2013–18*, Working Paper, Canberra.

Fox, J.E. and Jones, D. (2013) 'Migration, everyday life and the ethnicity bias', *Ethnicities*, 13: 385–400.

Fraser, N. (1989) 'Talking about needs: interpretive contests as political conflicts in welfare-state societies', *Ethics*, 99(2): 291–313.

Fraser, N. and Gordon, L. (1994) '"Dependency" demystified: inscriptions of power in a keyword of the welfare state', *Social Politics: International Studies in Gender, State & Society*, 1: 4–31.

Fraser, N. and Honneth, A. (2003) *Redistribution or Recognition? A Political-Philosophical Exchange*, London and New York: Verso Books.

Frost, L. and Hoggett, P. (2008) 'Human agency and social suffering', *Critical Social Policy*, 28: 438–60.

Furedi, F. (2008) 'Fear and security: a vulnerability-led policy response', *Social Policy & Administration*, 42: 645–61.

Garthwaite, K. (2016) 'The perfect fit? Being both volunteer and ethnographer in a UK foodbank', *Journal of Organizational Ethnography*, 5: 60–71.

Gazso, A., Baker Collins, S., Smith-Carrier, T. and Smith, C. (2020) 'The generationing of social assistance receipt and "welfare dependency" in Ontario, Canada', *Social Problems*, 67: 585–601.

Gibson, L. (2010) ' "Who you is?" Work and identity in Aboriginal New South Wales', in I. Keen (ed) *Indigenous Participation in Australian Economies: Historical and Anthropological Perspectives*, Canberra: ANU E Press, pp 127–39.

Giddens, A. (1998) *The Third Way: The Renewal of Social Democracy*, Cambridge, MA: Polity Press.

Gill, N., Singleton, V. and Waterton, C. (2017) 'The politics of policy practices', *The Sociological Review*, 65: 3–19.

Goffman, I. (1968) *Stigma: Notes on the Management of a Spoiled Identity*, Harmondsworth: Pelican.

Gray, C. (2019) 'The implementation and impact of National's welfare conditionality in an international context', *New Zealand Sociology*, 34: 71–92.

Hage, G. (1998) 'Evil white nationalists 1: the function of the hand in the execution of nationalist practices', in G. Hage (ed) *White Nation: Fantasies of White Supremacy in a Multicultural Australia*, Annandale, NSW: Pluto Press, pp 27–47.

Hage, G. (2001) 'Polluting memories: migration and colonial responsibility in Australia', in M. Morris and B. de Bary (eds) *"Race" Panic and the Memory of Migration*, Hong Kong: Hong Kong University Press, pp 333–62.

Hage, G. (2002) 'Multiculturalism and white paranoia in Australia', *Journal of International Migration and Integration*, 3: 417–37.

Hage, G. (2003) *Against Paranoid Nationalism: Searching for Hope in a Shrinking Society*, Annandale, NSW: Pluto Press.

Hage, G. (2012) 'Responsibility in the Lebanese transnational family', in G. Hage and R. Eckersley (eds) *Responsibility*, Melbourne, VIC: Melbourne University Press, pp 111–27.

Hall, T. and Smith, R.J. (2015) 'Care and repair and the politics of urban kindness', *Sociology*, 49: 3–18.

Harris, P. (2001) 'From relief to mutual obligation: welfare rationalities and unemployment in 20th-century Australia', *Journal of Sociology*, 37: 5–26.

Harrison, E. (2012) 'Bouncing back? Recession, resilience and everyday lives', *Critical Social Policy*, 33: 97–113.

Hillel, I. (2020) *Holes in the Social Safety Net: Poverty, Inequality and Social Assistance in Canada*, CSLS Research Report, Ottawa, ON.

Hockey, J. (2014) 'Budget 2014–15', Australian Government.

Hockey, J. and Forsey, M. (2012) 'Ethnography is not participant observation: reflections on the interview as participatory qualitative research', in: J. Skinner (ed) *The Interview: An Ethnographic Approach*, Milton Park: Taylor & Francis, pp 69–87.

Hoggett, P. (2000) *Emotional Life and the Politics of Welfare*, Basingstoke: Macmillan.

Hoggett, P. (2001) 'Agency, rationality and social policy', *Journal of Social Policy*, 30: 37–56.

Holmes, H. (2019) 'Unpicking contemporary thrift: getting on and getting by in everyday life', *The Sociological Review*, 67: 126–42.

Honneth, A. (1995) *The Struggle for Recognition: The Moral Grammar of Social Conflicts*, Cambridge, MA: Polity Press.

Humpage, L. (2010) 'Revisioning comparative welfare state studies: an "indigenous dimension"', *Policy Studies*, 31: 539–57.

Humpage, L. (2016) 'Income management in New Zealand and Australia: differently framed but similarly problematic for Indigenous peoples', *Critical Social Policy*, 36: 551–71.

Humpage, L., Staines, Z., Marston, G., Peterie, M., Bielefeld, S. and Mendes, P. (2020) 'The complexity of convergence: a multi-dimensional analysis of compulsory income management and social investment in New Zealand and Australia', *Policy Studies*, 43(4): 676–95.

Isin, E.F., Brodie, J., Juteau, D. and Stasiulis, D. (2008) 'Recasting the social in citizenship', in E.F. Isin (ed) *Recasting the Social in Citizenship*, Toronto: University of Toronto Press, pp 3–19.

Jacobs, K., Atkinson, R., Peisker, V.C., Berry, M. and Dalton, T. (2010) *What Future for Public Housing? A Critical Analysis*, AHURI Final Report, Melbourne, VIC: Australian Housing and Urban Research Institute.

Jakubowicz, A. (1989) 'The state and the welfare of immigrants in Australia', *Ethnic and Racial Studies*, 12: 1–35.

Jansen, B.J. (2008) 'Between vulnerability and assertiveness: negotiating resettlement in Kakuma refugee camp, Kenya', *African Affairs*, 107: 569–87.

Jordan, K. and Altman, J. (2016) 'From welfare to work, or work to welfare?', in K. Jordan and J. Altman (eds) *Better than Welfare? Work and Livelihoods for Indigenous Australians after CDEP*, Canberra, ACT: Australian National University Press, pp 1–29.

Karp, P. (2021) 'ATO won't pursue $180m in jobkeeper paid to ineligible businesses due to "honest mistakes"', *The Guardian*, 10 September.

Kenny, S. and Clarke, M. (2010) 'Introduction', in S. Kenny and M. Clarke (eds) *Challenging Capacity Building: Comparative Perspectives*, Hampshire and New York: Palgrave Macmillan, pp 1–20.

Kingfisher, C. (2013) *A Policy Travelogue: Tracing Welfare Reform in Aotearoa/ New Zealand and Canada*, New York and Oxford: Berghahn Books.

Kirmani, N. and Zaidi, S. (2010) *The Role of Faith in the Charity and Development Sector in Karachi and Sindh, Pakistan*, Religion and Development, International Development Department, University of Birmingham.

Klein, E. (2020) 'Why is the government trying to make the cashless debit card permanent? Research shows it does not work', *The Conversation*, 12 November.

Klein, E. (2021) 'Missing the value of care', *Arena*, 6.

Koleth, E. (2010) *Multiculturalism: A Review of Australian Policy Statements and Recent Debates in Australia and Overseas*, Parliamentary Library Research Paper, Canberra: Department of Parliamentary Services.

Komter, A.E. (2005) *Social Solidarity and the Gift*, Cambridge: Cambridge University Press.

Kowal, E. (2008) 'The politics of the gap: Indigenous Australians, liberal multiculturalism, and the end of the self-determination era', *American Anthropologist*, 110: 338–48.

Lahire, B. (2011) *The Plural Actor*, Cambridge: Polity.

Lamont, M. (2000) *The Dignity of Working Men: Morality and the Boundaries of Race, Class, and Immigration*, New York: Russell Sage Foundation.

Lamont, M. and Small, M.L. (2008) 'How culture matters: enriching our understanding of poverty', in A.C. Lin and D.R. Harris (eds) *The Colors of Poverty: Why Racial and Ethnic Disparities Persist*, New York: Russell Sage Foundation, pp 76–102.

Lea, T. (2012) 'When looking for anarchy, look to the state: fantasies of regulation in forcing disorder within the Australian Indigenous estate', *Critique of Anthropology*, 32: 109–24.

Leonard, R. and Onyx, J. (2004) *Social Capital and Community Building: Spinning Straw into Gold*, London: Janus Publishing.

Li, J., Brown, L., La, A.H., Miranti, R. and Vidyattama, Y. (2019) 'Inequalities in standards of living: evidence for improved income support for people with disability', Canberra: NATSEM, University of Canberra.

Liamputtong, P. (2007) *Researching the Vulnerable: A Guide to Sensitive Research Methods*, London: SAGE.

Lipsky, M. (2010) *Street-Level Bureaucracy: Dilemmas of the Individual in Public Services*, New York: Russell Sage Foundation.

Lister, R. (2004) *Poverty*, Cambridge: Polity Press.

Lister, R. (2015) '"To count for nothing": poverty beyond the statistics', *Journal of the British Academy*, 3: 139–65.

Lowe, J. (2015) 'Multiculturalism and its exclusions in New Zealand: the case for cosmopolitanism and indigenous rights', *Inter-Asia Cultural Studies*, 16: 496–512.

Lucashenko, M. (2013) 'Sinking below sight', *Griffith Review*, 41. Available from: www.griffithreview.com/articles/sinking-below-sight

MacDonald, G. (2000) 'Economies and personhood: demand sharing among the Wiradjuri of New South Wales', in: G.W. Wenzel, G. Hovelsrud-Broda and N. Kishigami (eds) *The Social Economy of Sharing: Resource Allocation and Modern Hunter-Gatherers*, Osaka: National Museum of Ethnology, pp 87–111.

Mackenzie, C., Rogers, W. and Dodds, S. (2014) 'Introduction: what is vulnerability, and why does it matter for moral theory?' in C. Mackenzie, W. Rogers and S. Dodds (eds) *Vulnerability: New Essays in Ethics and Feminist Philosophy*, New York and Oxford: Oxford University Press, pp 1–35.

Marks, K. (2012) 'Green card', *The Monthly*, 15–17.

Marshall, T.H. (1977) 'Citizenship and social class', in T.H. Marshall (ed) *Class, Citizenship and Social Development: Essays by T.H. Marshall*, Chicago, IL: University of Chicago Press, pp 71–134.

Marston, G. and McDonald, C. (2012) 'Getting beyond "heroic agency" in conceptualising social workers as policy actors in the twenty-first century', *British Journal of Social Work*, 42: 1022–38.

McClure Review (2015) *A New System for Better Employment and Social Outcomes, Final Report*. Report of the Reference Group on Welfare Reform to the Minister for Social Services. Australian Government, Department of Social Services, Canberra.

McCormack, K. (2004) 'Resisting the welfare mother: the power of welfare discourse and tactics of resistance', *Critical Sociology*, 30: 355–83.

McDonald, C. and Marston, G. (2006) 'Room to move? Professional discretion at the frontline of welfare-to-work', *Australian Journal of Social Issues*, 41: 171–82.

McKay, F.H. and Dunn, M. (2015) 'Food security among asylum seekers in Melbourne', *Australian and New Zealand Journal of Public Health*, 39: 344–9.

McKenzie, L. (2015) *Getting By: Estates, Class and Culture in Austerity Britain*, Bristol: Policy Press.

Mead, L.M. (1986) *Beyond Entitlement: The Social Obligations of Citizenship*, New York: Free Press.

Mead, L.M. (1997) 'The rise of paternalism', in L.M. Mead (ed) *The New Paternalism: Supervisory Approaches to Poverty*, Washington, DC: Brookings Institution Press, pp 1–38.

Meagher, G., and Healy, K. (2005) *Who Cares? Volume 1: A Profile of Care Workers in Australia's Community Services Industries*, Australian Council of Social Services (ACOSS) Papers, 93(1).

Mendes, P. (2009) 'Retrenching or renovating the Australian welfare state: the paradox of the Howard government's neo-liberalism', *International Journal of Social Welfare*, 18: 102–10.

Midgley, J. (2018) '"You were a lifesaver": encountering the potentials of vulnerability and self-care in a community café', *Ethics and Social Welfare*, 12: 49–64.

Millar, K. (2014) 'The precarious present: wageless labor and disrupted life in Rio de Janeiro, Brazil', *Cultural Anthropology*, 29: 32–53.

Mills, C. and Klein, E. (2021) 'Affective technologies of welfare deterrence in Australia and the United Kingdom', *Economy and Society*, 50: 397–422.

Misztal, B.A. (2011) *The Challenges of Vulnerability: In Search of Strategies for a Less Vulnerable Social Life*, Hampshire and New York: Palgrave Macmillan.

Mitchell, E. (2022) 'More than making do: towards a generative account of getting by on welfare benefits', *Sociology*, 56(3): 487–503

Mitchell, E. and Vincent, E. (2021) 'The shame of welfare? Lived experiences of welfare and culturally inflected experiences of shame', *Emotion, Space and Society*, 41: 1–8.

Moran, A. (2017) *The Public Life of Australian Multiculturalism: Building a Diverse Nation*, Cham, Switzerland: Palgrave Macmillan.

Moreton-Robinson, A. (2003) 'I still call Australia home: Indigenous belonging and place in a white postcolonizing society', in S. Ahmed, C. Castañeda, A.-M. Fortier and M. Sheller (eds) *Uprootings/ Regroundings: Questions of Home and Migration*, Oxford: Berg, pp 23–40.

Morris, A., Wilson, S. and Soldadic, K. (2015) 'Doing the "hard yakka": implications of Australia's workfare policies for disabled people', in C. Grover and L. Piggott (eds) *Disabled People, Work and Welfare: Is Employment Really the Answer?*, Bristol: Policy Press, pp 43–65.

Murphy, J. (2011) *A Decent Provision: Australian Welfare Policy, 1870 to 1949*, Abingdon: Routledge.

Murphy, J. (2013) 'Conditional inclusion: Aborigines and welfare rights in Australia, 1900–47', *Australian Historical Studies*, 44: 206–26.

Murphy, J., Murry, S., Chalmers, J., Martin, S. and Marston, G. (2011) *Half a Citizen: Life on Welfare in Australia*, Crows Nest, NSW: Allen & Unwin.

Murray, C. (1990) *The Emerging British Underclass*, London: Institute of Economic Affairs.

Newman, J. (2010) 'Towards a pedagogical state? Summoning the "empowered" citizen', *Citizenship Studies*, 14: 711–23.

O'Sullivan, S., McGann, M. and Considine, M. (2021) *Buying and Selling the Poor: Inside Australia's Privatised Welfare-to-Work Market*, Camperdown, NSW: Sydney University Press.

Offer, S. (2012) 'The burden of reciprocity: processes of exclusion and withdrawal from personal networks among low-income families', *Current Sociology*, 60: 788–805.

Orthner, D.K., Jones-Sanpei, H. and Williamson, S. (2004) 'The resilience and strengths of low-income families', *Family Relations*, 53: 159–67.

Ortner, S.B. (2001) 'Specifying agency: the Comaroffs and their critics', *Interventions*, 3: 76–84.

Osella, C. and Osella, F. (2006) 'Once upon a time in the West? Stories of migration and modernity from Kerala, South India', *Journal of the Royal Anthropological Institute*, 12: 569–88.

Osella, F. and Osella, C. (2000) 'Migration, money and masculinity in Kerala', *Journal of the Royal Anthropological Institute*, 6: 117–33.

Papillon, M. (2015) 'Playing catch-up with ghosts: income assistance for First Nations on reserves', in D. Béland and P.-M. Daigneault (eds) *Welfare Reform in Canada: Provincial Social Assistance in Comparative Perspective*, Toronto: University of Toronto Press, pp 323–38.

Parsell, C., Clarke, A. and Perales, F. (2022) *Charity and Poverty in Advanced Welfare States*, Abingdon: Routledge.

Patrick, R. (2017a) *For Whose Benefit? The Everyday Realities of Welfare Reform*, Bristol: Policy Press.

Patrick, R. (2017b) 'Wither social citizenship? Lived experiences of citizenship in/exclusion for recipients of out-of-work benefits', *Social Policy and Society*, 16: 293–304.

Pearson, N. (2000) *Our Right to Take Responsibility*, Cairns, QLD: Noel Pearson and Associates.

Peel, M. (2003) *The Lowest Rung: Voices of Australian Poverty*, Cambridge and New York: Cambridge University Press.

Peterie, M., Bielefeld, S., Marston, G., Mendes, P. and Humpage, L. (2020) 'Compulsory income management: combatting or compounding the underlying causes of homelessness?', *Australian Journal of Social Issues*, 55: 61–72.

Peterie, M., Ramia, G., Marston, G. and Patulny, R. (2019) 'Emotional compliance and emotion as resistance: shame and anger among the long-term unemployed', *Work, Employment and Society*, 33: 794–811.

Pierson, C. and Humpage, L. (2016) 'Coming together or drifting apart? Income maintenance in Australia, New Zealand, and the United Kingdom', *Politics and Policy* 44: 261–93.

Piven, F.F. and Cloward, R.A. (1972) *Regulating the Poor: The Functions of Public Welfare*, New York: Vintage Books.

Probyn, E. (2004) 'Everyday shame', *Cultural Studies*, 18: 328–49.

Rattan, R. and Mountain, W. (2016) 'Indigenous incarceration in Australia at a glance', *The Conversation*, 15 April.

Redmond, G., Main, G., O'Donnell, A.W., Skattebol, J., Woodman, R., Mooney, A. et al (2022) 'Who excludes? Young people's experience of social exclusion', *Journal of Social Policy*, 1–24.

Rosen, S. (1996) *Bankstown: A Sense of Identity*, Sydney: Hale and Iremonger.

Rowse, T. (1998) 'Indigenous citizenship and self-determination: the problem of shared responsibilities', in N. Peterson and W. Sanders (eds) *Citizenship and Indigenous Australians: Changing Conceptions and Possibilities*, Cambridge: Cambridge University Press, pp 79–100.

Saldaña, J. (2009) *The Coding Manual for Qualitative Researchers*, Thousand Oaks: SAGE

Sanders, W. (2008) *Equality and Difference Arguments in Australian Indigenous Affairs: Examples from Income Support and Housing*, Australian National University, Centre for Aboriginal Economic Policy Research.

Sanders, W. and Hunt, J. (2010) 'Sorry, but the Indigenous affairs revolution continues', in C. Aulich and M. Evans (eds) *The Rudd Government: Australian Commonwealth Administration 2007–2010*, Canberra, VIC: ANU E Press, pp 221–40.

Saunders, P. (2004) *Australia's Welfare Habit and How to Kick It*, Sydney: Duffy and Snellgrove/Centre for Independent Studies

Saunders, P. (2007) 'The costs of disability and the incidence of poverty', *Australian Journal of Social Issues*, 42: 461.

Saunders, P. (2011) *Down and Out: Poverty and Exclusion in Australia*, Bristol: Policy Press.

Sayer, A. (2005) *The Moral Significance of Class*, Cambridge: Cambridge University Press.

Seccombe, K. (2002) '"Beating the odds" versus "changing the odds": poverty, resilience, and family policy', *Journal of Marriage and Family*, 64: 384–94.

Sen, A. (1999) *Development as Freedom*, Oxford: Oxford University Press.

Sennett, R. (2003) *Respect: The Formation of Character in an Age of Inequality*, London and New York: Penguin Books.

Sennett, R. and Cobb, J. (1972) *The Hidden Injuries of Class*, Cambridge: Cambridge University Press.

Shaver, S. (2007) 'Culture, multiculturalism and the welfare state citizenship', *Annual Meeting of International Sociological Association Research Committee 19 on Poverty, Social Welfare and Social Policy, 'Social Policy in a Globalizing World: Developing a North-South Dialogue'*, Florence.

Shildrick, T. and MacDonald, R. (2013) 'Poverty talk: how people experiencing poverty deny their poverty and why they blame "the poor"', *The Sociological Review*, 61: 285–303.

Shildrick, T., MacDonald, R., Furlong, A., Roden, J. and Crow, R. (2012) *Are 'Cultures of Worklessness' Passed Down the Generations?*, York: Joseph Rowntree Foundation.

Shutes, I. (2016) 'Work-related conditionality and the access to social benefits of national citizens, EU and non-EU citizens', *Journal of Social Policy*, 45: 691–707.

Sinding, C. and Aronson, J. (2003) 'Exposing failures, unsettling accommodations: tensions in interview practice', *Qualitative Research*, 3: 95–117.

Sivey, P. (2016) 'How much?! Seeing private specialists often costs more than you bargained for,' *The Conversation*, 16 March.

Smith-Carrier, T. (2017) 'Reproducing social conditions of poverty: a critical feminist analysis of social assistance participation in Ontario, Canada', *Journal of Women, Politics & Policy*, 38: 498–521.

Smits, K. (2011) 'Justifying multiculturalism: social justice, diversity and national identity in Australia and New Zealand', *Australian Journal of Political Science*, 46: 87–103.

Smyth, P. (2011) 'The British social policy legacy in Australia', in J. Midgley and P. Piachaud (eds) *Colonialism and Welfare: Social Policy and the British Imperial Legacy*, Cheltenham: Edward Elgar Publishing, pp 175–88.

Soldadic, K., Bowman, D., Mupandemunda, M. and McGee, P. (2021) *Dead Ends: How Our Social Security System Is Failing People with Partial Capacity to Work*, Fitzroy, VIC: Brotherhood of St Laurence.

Spies-Butcher, B. (2014) 'Welfare reform', in C. Miller and L. Orchard (eds) *Australian Public Policy: Progressive Ideas in the Neoliberal Ascendency*, Bristol: Policy Press, pp 81–96.

Staines, Z., Moore, C., Marston, G. and Humpage, L. (2021) 'Big data and poverty governance under Australia and Aotearoa/New Zealand's "social investment" policies', *Australian Journal of Social Issues*, 56: 157–72.

Stanley, E. and De Froideville, S.M. (2020) 'From vulnerability to risk: consolidating state interventions towards Māori children and young people in New Zealand', *Critical Social Policy*, 40: 526–45.

Stinson, H. (2019) 'Supporting people? Universal Credit, conditionality and the recalibration of vulnerability', in P. Dwyer (ed) *Dealing with Welfare Conditionality: Implementation and Effects*, Bristol: Policy Press, pp 15–40.

Strakosch, E. (2015) *Neoliberal Indigenous Policy: Settler Colonialism and the 'Post-Welfare' State*, Hampshire and New York: Palgrave Macmillan.

Stringer, R. (2014) 'Vulnerability after wounding: feminism, rape law and the differend', in R. Stringer (ed) *Knowing Victims: Feminism, Agency and Victim Politics in Neoliberal Times*, London: Taylor & Francis, pp 57–86.

Strong, S. (2021) 'Towards a geographical account of shame: foodbanks, austerity, and the spaces of austere affective governmentality', *Transactions of the institute of British Geographers*, 46: 73–86.

Tavan, G. (2012) 'No going back? Australian multiculturalism as a path-dependent process', *Australian Journal of Political Science*, 47: 547–61.

Taylor, D.R., Gray, M. and Stanton, D. (2016) 'New conditionality in Australian social security policy', *Australian Journal of Social Issues*, 51: 3–26.

Thornton, D., Bowman, D. and Mallett, S. (2020) *Safety Net to Poverty Trap? The Twentieth-Century Origins of Australia's Uneven Social Security System*, Fitzroy, VIC: Brotherhood of St Laurence.

Thrift, N. (2005) 'But malice aforethought: cities and the natural history of hatred', *Transactions of the institute of British Geographers*, 30: 133–50.

Tingle, L. (2012) *Great Expectations: Government, Entitlement and an Angry Nation*, Collingwood, VIC: Black Inc.

Tracy, S.J. (2010) 'Qualitative quality: eight "big-tent" criteria for excellent qualitative research', *Qualitative Inquiry*, 16: 837–51.

Tuck, E. (2009) 'Suspending damage: a letter to communities', *Harvard Educational Review*, 79: 409–28.

Tyler, I. and Slater, T. (2018) 'Rethinking the sociology of stigma', *The Sociological Review*, 66: 721–43.

Ungar, M. (2008) 'Resilience across cultures', *British Journal of Social Policy*, 38: 218–35.

van Kooy, J. and Ward, J. (2019) *An Unnecessary Penalty: Economic Impacts of Changes to the Status Resolution Support Services*, Surry Hills: Refugee Council of Australia. Available from: https://www.refugeecouncil.org.au/srss-economic-penalty/

Vasta, E. (2004) 'Community, the state and the deserving citizen: Pacific Islanders in Australia', *Journal of Ethnic and Migration Studies*, 30: 195–213.

Vincent, E. (2021) 'Look after them? Gender, care and welfare reform in Aboriginal Australia', *Ethnos*, pp 1–20.

Vincent, E. (2023) *Who Cares? Life on Welfare in Australia*, Carlton, VIC: Melbourne University Press.

Walker, R., Kyomuhendo, G.B., Chase, E., Choudhry, S., Gubrium, E., Yongmie Nicola, J. et al (2013) 'Poverty in global perspective: is shame a common denominator?', *Journal of Social Policy*, 42: 215–33.

Walsh, J.P. (2014) 'The marketization of multiculturalism: neoliberal restructuring and cultural difference in Australia', *Ethnic and Racial Studies*, 37: 280–301.

Walter, M. (2009) 'An economy of poverty? Power and the domain of Aboriginality', *International Journal of Critical Indigenous Studies*, 2: 2–14.

Watson, N. (2010) 'Northern Territory emergency response: the more things change, the more they stay the same', *Alberta Law Review*, 48: 905.

Watts, B. and Fitzpatrick, S. (2018) *Welfare Conditionality*, London: Routledge.

Werdal, T. and Mitchell, L.M. (2018) '"Looking out for each other": street-involved youth's perspectives on friendship', *Anthropologica*, 60: 314–26.

White, M. (1999) 'PM's 20-year target to end poverty', *The Guardian*, 19 March.

Whiteford, P. and Bradbury, B. (2021) 'The $50 boost to Job Seeker will take Australia's payment from the lowest in the OECD to the second-lowest after Greece', *The Conversation*, 23 February.

Wilson, S., Spies-Butcher, B. and Stebbing, A. (2009) 'Targets and taxes: explaining the welfare orientations of the Australian public', *Social Policy & Administration*, 43: 508–25.

Wilson, S., Spies-Butcher, B., Stebbing, A. and St John, S. (2013) 'Wage-earners' welfare after economic reform: refurbishing, retrenching or hollowing out social protection in Australia and New Zealand?', *Social Policy & Administration*, 47: 623–46.

Wong, Y. and Tsai, J. (2007) 'Cultural models of shame and guilt', in J. Tracy, R. Robins and J. Tangney (eds) *The Self-Conscious Emotions: Theory and Research*, New York: The Guilford Press, pp 209–223.

Wright, S., Marston, G. and McDonald, C. (2011) 'The role of non-profit organizations in the mixed economy of welfare-to-work in the UK and Australia', *Social Policy & Administration*, 45: 299–318.

Yamanouchi, Y. (2010) '"Kinship, organisations and wannabes": Aboriginal identity negotiation in south-western Sydney', *Oceania*, 80(2): 216–28.

Index

References to tables appear in **bold** type;
references to endnotes show both the page
number and the note number (117n1).